UNDERSTANDING
THE BASIC PRINCIPLES OF
ISLAM

UNDERSTANDING

THE BASIC PRINCIPLES OF

ISLAM

Ömer A. Ergi

TUGHRA
BOOKS

New Jersey

21 20 19 18   2 3 4 5

Published by Tughra Books
345 Clifton Ave., Clifton,
NJ, 07011, USA

www.tughrabooks.com

Library of Congress Cataloging-in-Publication Data

Ergi, Ömer A.
Understanding the basic principles of Islam / Ömer A. Ergi.
134 p. ; 20 cm.
ISBN: 978-1-59784-245-7 (pbk. : alk. paper)
BP161.3 .E74 2012
2012404507

ISBN: 978-1-59784-245-7
Printed in Canada

CONTENTS

FAITH

F aith is a kernel implanted into the heart of every human being by the Almighty Creator. It is up to the individual to cultivate and nurture it so that it may transform into a spiritual tree which would eventually bear eternal fruits. Through faith, the human heart attains its true form which evidently is a luminous mirror that reflects the most Beautiful Names of Allah.

Faith is a powerful light that illuminates one's internal and external realms. It is a light that feeds on sincerity and acquires its energy from worship. This unique metaphysical light is so apparent that it could even be detected on the face of a believer in the form of a mysterious radiant glow.

Faith is the very reason for human existence. Without faith human beings cannot be distinguished from rest of the living species whose physical constituents do not differ in fundamental nature. It is faith that makes human being a human being. Through faith and worship human beings establish an indissoluble connection between themselves and their Maker.

Faith brings hope and meaning to human life. Without faith, life becomes a battle ground where every human being endures an ephemeral struggle of survival which eventually concludes with the inevitable truth defined as death. For those who do not have faith, death is the absolute termination of their very existence. Therefore, it is a horrible reality that nonbelievers wish to avoid for as long as possible. However, for those who have faith, death is not the end, but the very beginning. It is merely a doorway which opens to an eternal life, a place of reunion and a realm of indulgence. Consequently, the presumed dark face of death can only be illuminated with the everlasting light of faith. Through faith, even death becomes meaningful.

Hearts and minds of those who have faith are in constant process of expansion. Their vision is not restricted by the boundaries of the physical universe. It stretches beyond and into a realm of metaphysics that holds infinite possibilities. Like a black hole, faith punctures a hole into the fabric of the physical world of materialism and opens a window to eternal hope. It is through this window, mortals can get a glimpse of immortality as they gaze into the realm of metaphysics.

Faith is the ultimate truth veiled by physical causes and materialistic rationale. Those who are fortunate enough to discover the authentic truth that exists behind the veil of materialism will achieve eternal happiness, serenity, peace and contentment.

The purpose of being human can only be comprehended through faith. Without question, human beings were created in a way that distinguishes them from rest of the creation. Human desires are endless and their fears and reservations are countless. These intriguing emotions cannot be satisfied by physical means. Attempting to gratify the carnal desires of a human being is similar to trying to quench the thirst of a dehydrated person by offering bottles of seawater. Human beings were created for eternity; therefore, the human soul will never be content with impermanent pleasures, transient kingdoms and temporary wealth. The absolute gratification and contentment that the human soul seeks can only be attained through faith. Since human beings were created for perpetuity, they can only be satisfied with eternity.

Question: What is faith and how does one embrace it?

Answer: Faith is the greatest truth in the universe and human beings are equipped with the necessary tools to investigate and discover this truth. Two of the most important truth-seeking tools bestowed upon human beings are the intellect and the heart. Study of natural sciences is the nourishment of the intellect and study of religious knowledge is the light of the heart. It is through the amalgamation of these two imperative studies that the ultimate truth will emerge. Consequently, the emerging facts will lead to faith. When truly embraced, faith will elevate its bearer from a level of a species of mammal to the echelon of being human, or perhaps to the rank of a king. Without faith, a human being will be considered as nothing but a vicious hominid that preys on many other species in order to survive.

So, faith is the most important element that separates us from rest of Allah's creation. It transforms human beings into dignified representatives of Allah's creation and also honored vicegerents of the Almighty. Moreover, it converts human beings into enthusiastic art-lovers who observe and praise Allah's magnificent creation. Faith is a spiritual ecstasy experienced only by those who possess it. Not only does it establish a spiritual contentment in one's heart but it also brings peace and tranquility to one's life.

A true believer observes nature through the binoculars of faith. Suddenly, everything takes a new meaning and all matter assumes a purpose to exist. In the eyes of a believer, they are all Allah's servants that exist to perform various most significant duties. And the universe is a great book published by the Almighty Author. Everything in the universe is a Divine sign and everything is a word from Him. Reading this great book, along with the holy book brought down to His beloved Messenger will lead human beings to true faith. Consequently, such faith, obtained through analytical knowledge, will eventually lead to total submission and worship.

Faith is the quintessence of religion. Without faith, rituals and rites can only be considered as habitual acts or customs. It is faith that gives meaning to practice. Through faith, good deeds attain a Divine purpose and increase drastically in value. In other words, the intention of pleasing Allah transforms even the simplest of acts into worship. Once the believer begins to display his faith through worship, he is on the path to fulfilling the purpose of his very existence.

In conclusion, faith is the greatest gift bestowed upon humanity. It is more precious than the entire universe and its wealth. Only those who possess true faith may compre-hend the semantics of this statement…

The concept of belief in Islam is based on complete faith. Faith cannot be divided or embraced partially. In Islamic terminology, faith is defined as *Iman* and it con-sists of six essential principles. These six principles are defined as the 'articles of faith'. Belief in Allah, belief in angels, belief in Divine Books, belief in the Prophets, belief in the Day of Judgment and belief in destiny are the six articles of faith. An individual who rejects any one of these articles will not be regarded as a Muslim even if he/she accepts all of the other five. Therefore, a complete faith can only be obtained by embracing all of the articles of faith and then declaring that "There is no deity but Allah, and Muhammad is His servant and Messenger."

Islamic scholars propose that there are two types of faith.

1. Faith through cultural heritage
2. Faith through analytical scrutiny

Faith through heritage means embracing religion due to an influence from parents, community, society or tradi-tion. Although, this type of faith is still acceptable, it is weak and unless it is strengthened through knowledge and worship, it can be destabilized with the slightest of doubts. Faith through analytical scrutiny, on the other hand, is strong because it is obtained through knowledge, wisdom, logic and experience. This type of faith is embraced by the intellect and the soul; with Allah's aid such faith will be eternal. Of course, both paths mentioned above are related to human freewill hence they are chosen through the use of intellect, comprehension or sometimes through social persuasion. However, the reality is obtaining true faith cannot be solely based on these paths. The defined paths can only be considered as means to obtain faith, because it is Allah Himself who places human beings onto the right path and blesses their hearts with faith. In Islam this is called, *hidayah* (guidance towards the path of righteousness). Indeed, Allah puts *hidayah* into the hearts of human beings but one must also remember that this has to be earned through intention, sincerity, effort, spirituality and intellect.

In conclusion, it is imperative that faith is obtained and strengthened through the study of religious literature, natural sciences and practice. It is essential that Muslims acknowledge the fact that the Almighty Allah has sent two great books which lead to attaining an ideal faith. These two books are: the Holy Qur'an and the great book of the universe.

BASIC PRINCIPLES OF ISLAM

R eligion of Islam is based on two sets of imperative articles and pillars:
- Articles of Faith
- Pillars of Islam

There are six articles of faith and *mu'min,* a believer is obligated to embrace and have complete faith in all of the six articles. Before we elucidate the profundity of the six articles of faith, let us first explain what a person needs to do, in order to embrace Islam. A person must first declare that he /she has faith in Islam by reciting the testimony of faith. The testimony of faith is declared by making the following statement:

أَشْهَدُ أَنْ لَا إِلَهَ إِلَّا اللهُ وَأَشْهَدُ أَنَّ مُحَمَّدًا عَبْدُهُ وَرَسُولُهُ

Ashhadu alla ilaha illa Allah, wa ashhadu anna Muhammadan abduhu wa Rasuluhu.

This is called *Shahadah* and the English translation of *Shahadah* is "I testify that there is no deity but Allah, and I testify that Muhammad is the servant and Messenger of Allah". There is one important issue here that needs to be clarified and that is "Why do Muslims use the term Allah instead of Allah?"

In the Arabic language, *Ilah* is the English version of the word God. It means 'something that is worshipped'.

However, just as in the English language, the word god, *Ilah* can be made plural and it can be defined as male or female. The word *"Allah"* on the other hand, does not have a plural form and it cannot be associated with gender. Unlike, other personal names in Arabic, Allah is definite and absolute hence it refers to one Supreme Being only. Although, "Allah" still means God, in Islam it is considered as the personal name of the One and Only God.

Conversely, there is no harm in using the term God as long as one uses the term with the pure intention of referring to the Almighty Allah. The most obvious distinction between the term God and Allah is that the term God is used as an attribute rather than a name. It means, "The creator and the supreme being that is worshipped." However, in Islam, Allah has many Attributes. For example, *Rahman* means the All-Merciful; *Rahim* means the All-Compassionate; *Karim* means the All-Munificent; *Hayy* means the All-Living; *Quddus* means the All-Pure and so on.

The second component of the testimony of faith is "I testify that Muhammad is the servant and Messenger of Allah". This means that the believer accepts and embraces the Divine truth that Prophet Muhammad, peace and blessings be upon him, is the servant and Messenger of Allah. He is the last Messenger of Allah who comes with Divine revelations to guide humanity onto the right path. This testimony is also an affirmation that the believer accepts the message conveyed by the Prophet and makes the pledge to follow and practice his religion.

Servanthood is the very purpose in the creation of human beings and the Prophet holds the highest rank of servanthood. Therefore, by declaring the testimony of faith, the believer also pledges to take Allah's Messenger as the principal guide to true servanthood.

Following this brief explanation, let us once again clarify the issue of taking the initial step in embracing Islam. In order to embrace Islam, one must first declare the testimony of faith with his or her tongue and accept it with the heart. However, a person cannot become a true believer until he/she has complete faith in the six articles of faith. So what are the six articles of faith? They are as follows:

- Belief in Allah
- Belief in Angels
- Belief in Divine Books
- Belief in Prophets
- Belief in the Day of Judgment
- Belief in Divine destiny

In the following chapters, each article of faith is explained clearly...

SIX ARTICLES OF FAITH

BELIEF IN ALLAH

The first and the foremost important article of faith is belief in Allah. The primary purpose in the creation of human beings is that they recognize the Almighty Creator and acknowledge His Might. Furthermore, this recognition must lead to submission and worship. Belief in Allah is the most important requirement of being human. In order to comprehend this notion one needs to examine the universe and his/her own very existence. The mystery of existence cannot be explained without a creator. In his, *Questions and Answers,* Fethullah Gülen explains:

> The existence of Allah is too evident to need any arguments. Some saintly scholars have stated that Allah Himself is more manifest than any other being, but those who lack insight cannot see Him. Others have said that He is concealed from direct perception because of His Self-manifestation's intensity.
>
> However, the great influence of positivism and materialism on science humanity makes it necessary to discuss such arguments. This way of thinking reduces existence to what can be directly perceived and thereby blinds itself to the invisible dimensions of existence, which are far more vast than the visible. Since we must strive to remove the veil drawn by materialism and positivism, we will review briefly

some of the traditional demonstrations for Allah's necessary existence.

Before doing so, it is worth reflecting upon the historical fact that, since the very beginning of human life, the overwhelming majority of humanity has believed in Allah's existence. This alone is enough to establish Allah's existence. Unbelievers cannot claim intellectual superiority over believers, for the latter contain many innovative scientists, scholars, researchers and, most importantly, saints and Prophets (the experts in this field). Also, people usually confuse the non-acceptance of something's existence with the acceptance of its non-existence. While the former is only a negation or a rejection, the latter is a judgment needing proof. No one has ever proven, and cannot prove, Allah's non-existence. In contrast, countless arguments prove His existence.[1]

As explained by Gülen, denying the existence of Allah cannot be based on any scientific evidence nor can it be proven. On the other hand, everything in the universe points to a creator. It is evident that physical matter is transitory hence the universe had a beginning. It is also evident that matter cannot create itself. When we observe the universe and nature around us, we realize that all matter—living and non-living—functions with purpose. There is design, harmony, beauty, laws and purpose in nature. Accordingly, it is quite logical to affirm that design indicates a designer; art indicates an artist; purpose indicates intelligence; program indicates a programmer and tempo-

---

[1] Fethullah Gülen, *Questions and Answers*, The Light Inc. 2000.

rary beauty points to eternal beauty. Basically, creation points to a creator.

Unfortunately, the argument of "I do not believe in something that I cannot see" has been around for hundreds of years. It is ironic that we still come across people who persist with this argument in spite of the developments achieved by modern science. Assuming that such argument is received, what is a blind person suppose to believe in? In reality, even individuals who possess the gift of vision, observe the world through a very tiny window. Human vision is extremely limited and cannot be used as a tool of denial. This example can be used for all human faculties. Our senses of scent, hearing, touch and taste are also quite limited. Therefore, one cannot deny the existence of something using the argument of "I cannot see, hear, smell, touch or taste it". There are millions of entities in the universe that we cannot see, hear, smell, touch or taste; yet, we detect their existence through scientific knowledge or reason. Denying the existence of Allah by using the argument of "I cannot see or detect Him" can be likened to a hypothetical argument made by a bacterium living in the intestines of man, claiming that "man does not exist because I cannot see him."

The existence of Allah is beyond doubt and one recognizes this fact through His art of creation. Talent of the artist is recognized through his art. For example, does not the painting of Mona Lisa point to Leonardo Da Vinci? It is quite obvious that art has beauty and purpose. It is exhibited so that intelligent beings would admire it and in turn acknowledge the talent behind it. When we examine the universe from the perspective of all scientific disciplines and from an artistic point of view, we realize that there is a common factor behind everything. Everything in existence is the product of the very same hand. There is perfection, beauty, symmetry, purpose, measurement and precision in all matter. Yet everything we observe exists in front of the veil of materialism. Our vision cannot penetrate the cloak of the materialistic realm.

Consequently, we try to interpret nature with our limited perception, yet everything that exists in front of the curtains point to a talented hand behind the stage. Let us explain this argument with an analogy:

Imagine that you are in a theatre, sitting amid a large audience. There is a stage in front of you and on stage there is a canvas, an artist's palette and various colors of paint. You can see a paintbrush jutting from behind the stage curtains. The handle of the brush is behind the curtains so it is not visible to you, but it is in motion. Before your very eyes, it dips into various colors of paint and moves onto the canvas. With every stroke you are viewing a masterpiece of art being created before your very eyes. All the components of this masterpiece are quite visible to you. However, discovering what exists behind the curtains is beyond your physical capability. This is when the ultimate question arises: Is it possible that the handle of the brush is floating in midair? How should we as the audience interpret this bizarre phenomenon realizing that we only have the means to study and analyze what is on stage?

Should we applaud the brush, the paint or the canvas? Or should we be thinking that there may be a great artist behind the curtains?

Without question, the magnificent art and complexity we observe in nature surpasses by far any human-made art or design. Are we not obligated to acknowledge the great designer that exists behind the veil of this physical universe? Furthermore, the mindboggling work done by this mysterious hand is not restricted to design alone. When we study nature, we observe tremendous power, incomprehensible precision, inexplicable compassion and unfathomable flow of sustenance. It is as if the entire universe was fine-tuned so that living beings, in particular the human race could exist and maintain its existence. From the requirements of the tiny stomach of an ant to countless needs of human beings, all sustenance is prepared by this merciful hand and serviced to all creatures that cannot otherwise obtain them. When nature is scrutinized with the intellect and the heart working in collaboration, it becomes quite obvious that the sun with its powerful ultraviolet rays, the atmosphere with its defined composition and the earth with its precise motion and structure, work in harmony so that life on earth could be preserved. Any intelligent individual would realize that the millions of occurrences needed for the continuation of life on earth do not take place by means of randomness or chance. A profound contemplation and deliberation on the origin of the universe will lead to the recognition of the Ultimate Power that exists behind the veil of materialism. Evidently, ascribing the origin of life to millions of random events that eventuate by means of blind chance would be quite illogical in comparison to ascribing everything to one Commander Who is the cause of all causes. This can be proven with a simple allegory:

Is it more logical to assign 100 generals to one soldier or one general to 100 soldiers? If we consider all matter in the universe as soldiers that function with certain laws and regulations, then assigning one general to everything would be reasonably logical. Otherwise, we would have quite a difficult task of explaining the perfect order and harmony that exists in nature and throughout the physical universe. Therefore, the design of the universe points to a great Designer and this designer is no other than the Almighty Allah.

This is precisely what the first article of faith requires of believers. Those who have embraced Islam must first recognize the Almighty Allah, the Great Designer, the All-Merciful. He has created the universe and His human servants so that they may recognize and acknowledge Him. He wished to be known hence the primary duty of humans is to acknowledge their Lord and submit to His will. Consequently, one cannot possess faith without belief in the One and Only Allah.

The concept of Allah in Islam, however, is quite unique. It is strictly monotheistic. Islam rejects all forms associations with Allah. Allah has no partners and He is other than His creation. Therefore, in Islam it is forbidden to assign a mother, son, daughter or any partner to Allah.

The notion of unity of Allah is described quite unambig-uously in the Holy Qur'an:

قُلْ هُوَ اللهُ اَحَدٌ ۚ اَللهُ الصَّمَدُ ۚ لَمْ يَلِدْ وَلَمْ يُولَدْ ۚ وَلَمْ يَكُنْ لَهُ كُفُواً اَحَدٌ

Say, "He is Allah, the One; Allah, the Eternal, Absolute;
He begets not, and nor is He begotten; and there is noth-
ing that can be compared to Him."[2]

Consequently, Allah cannot be associated with part-ners. He is One, but this concept of one is not a mathe-matical or numerical one. In Arabic, the term is *Ahad,* a unique one that cannot be compared to other ones. Math-ematical concepts of division, multiplication, subtraction and addition do not apply to this form of oneness. The concept of Allah in Islam also teaches us that He does not need anything yet everything needs Him. This means that He does not depend on anything, including space-time. Before the creation of the entire existence, there was noth-ing but Him. He is eternal in the past and in the future, therefore, He was not begotten nor does he beget. He is so unique that there is none like unto Him. This means that He cannot be compared with anything physical or metaphysical. Another most significant issue about the concept of Allah in Islam is His Omnipotence and Sover-eignty. Allah has absolute power over all existence. From the motions of sub-atomic particles to giant galaxies and from a bacterium to a blue whale, everything functions and lives through His power. Everything in nature, includ-

---

[2]   Qur'an: 112:1–4.

ing living organisms exist and maintain their existence through His supremacy and inspiration.

The laws of physics do not apply to Allah. One of the most fundamental laws of physics, *cause and effect* applies only to matter. Therefore, the question put forward by some nonbelievers:

If Allah created everything then who created Allah is not a valid question. There is no ration in the argument, because in philosophy one does not enter into a chain reaction. If one were to assume that the creator was created by another being, then the question would be who created him and so on. The problem won't be solved no matter how far one goes back. Then what is the logic in producing so many creators when One is capable of creating everything.

Let us explain this with an analogy: Imagine that you are sitting on a chair that has two back legs missing. You would obviously fall back. To prevent yourself from falling back, you have placed another chair at the rear-bottom the chair you are sitting on, but this chair also has two back legs missing. So once again you have a third chair supporting the second one at the back, but also with no back legs. No matter how far you go back or how many chairs you place—one after the other, if you are able to sit on the front chair without falling back, this means that at the very end there is a chair with four legs. Evidently, you need a chair that supports all the chairs yet does not need support. Then what use would you have for all the other chairs that cannot even support themselves?

This argument could be further strengthened with the following question: "what pulls the last wagon on a train?" The obvious response to this question is "the wagon in front of it." Then the next question would be: "What pulls that one?" The Answer would obviously be the wagon in front of that one. This line of questioning would continue until one comes to the locomotive. It would then be illogical to ask "what pulls the locomotive", because the locomotive is self powered. Philosophically, the argument of who created Allah would continue with a series of repeated questions. Such line of questioning would have to conclude at some point by accepting that there is a Allah who creates but does not need to be created. He is the All-Powerful, Eternal Allah.

In the study of the origin of matter, there is a point where an effect does not have a physical cause anymore. At this point we have to conclude that in order to exist, even physical laws needed to be created. Consequently, creation points to a Creator and this Creator cannot be similar to His creation. He is the All-Powerful, All-Knowing and Omnipotent Allah.

Another question that usually follows the one we have addressed above is:

If Allah Does Not Need Anything, Then Why Did He Create the Universe?

First of all, Allah created the universe because He is the Creator. How can He be the creator if He did not create? An attribute can only be true if it is performed or act out. For example, lawyer is an attribute of a person who practices law; a mountain climber is an attribute of a person who climbs mountains and so on... Can we assign the attribute of 'swimmer' to a person who does not know how to swim? This means that one needs to perform the act in order to possess the attribute. Therefore, Allah created the universe because He is the Creator. However, in relation to why Allah created the universe, the argument of necessity is not valid. The reason for this is necessity originates from deficiency. Allah cannot be associated with any form of deficiency. This means He does not need anything. So why did He then create the universe? There could be a billion reasons yet the human mind is incapable of comprehending the purpose behind the acts of Allah. Islamic scholars, however, suggested two major reasons for creation:

1. Allah wanted to be known

2. Allah created the universe out of compassion

In conclusion, the first article of faith in Islam is belief in Allah as His Names and Attributes are described explicitly in the Holy Qur'an...

BELIEF IN ANGELS

أَمَنَ الرَّسُولُ بِمَا أُنْزِلَ إِلَيْهِ مِنْ رَبِّهِ وَالْمُؤْمِنُونَ كُلٌّ أَمَنَ بِالله وَمَلَئِكَتِهِ وَكُتُبِهِ وَرُسُلِهِ

*The Messenger believes in what has been revealed to him
from his Lord, and so do the believers. All believe in Allah,
His Angels and His Messengers.*[3]

Belief in angels is the second article of the six essential principles of faith. In proximity, angels are the closest beings to the Almighty Allah. They are created out of *Nur* (pure light). Angels do not possess an animalistic side like humans, therefore, they do not have desires of their own, and neither do they eat or drink. Angels are the honored servants of Allah and they never disobey His exalted commands. They are constantly in the service of their eternal Master. Some angels worship Allah continuously as they stand in upright position, bowing position or prostration position. Some angels have ongoing individual duties, whereas some perform collective duties. There are angels called up on only in certain circumstances and there are those whose duties are limited to one single mission.

---

[3] Qur'an: 2:285.

Angels do not have a gender. They do not produce off-spring. Fundamental needs for human beings such as sustenance do not apply to angels. They are nourished through the act of worship and serving Allah. However, angels do possess intelligence and the power of reasoning. This is quite evident in many Qur'anic verses:

وَاِذْ قَالَ رَبُّكَ لِلْمَلٰئِكَةِ اِنِّى جَاعِلٌ فِى الْاَرْضِ خَلِيفَةً قَالُوا اَتَجْعَلُ فِيهَا مَنْ يُفْسِدُ فِيهَا وَيَسْفِكُ الدِّمَاءَ وَنَحْنُ نُسَبِّحُ بِحَمْدِكَ وَنُقَدِّسُ لَكَ قَالَ اِنِّى اَعْلَمُ مَا لَا تَعْلَمُونَ

…When your Lord said to the angels: "I am setting on the earth a vicegerent." The angels asked: "Will you set therein one who will cause disorder and corruption on it and shed blood, while we glorify You with Your praise (proclaiming that You are absolutely above having any defect and that all praise belongs to You exclusively), and declare that You alone are All-Holy and to be worshipped as Allah and Lord?" He said: "Surely I know what you do not know.[4]

It is clear from the verse above that angels were wondering about the purpose behind the creation of human beings, hence, they asked their Lord why He would create a being that would cause mischief and shed blood on earth. Following the creation of Adam, peace be upon him, Allah taught him the names of all things. Then He asked His angels to name these things, yet they could not. When Adam, peace be upon him, spoke and told them all the Names, Allah said:

قَالَ اَلَمْ اَقُلْ لَكُمْ اِنِّى اَعْلَمُ غَيْبَ السَّمٰوَاتِ وَالْاَرْضِ وَاَعْلَمُ مَا تُبْدُونَ وَمَا كُنْتُمْ تَكْتُمُونَ

---

[4] Qur'an: 2:30.

*Did I not tell you that I know the secrets of heaven and
earth, and I know what you reveal and what you conceal?*[5]

By the commandment of Allah, the angels then bowed
and prostrated before Adam, peace be upon him. The only
being who refused to bow down was *Iblis* (Satan). This
incident also teaches us that although Allah has given angels
the ability to question and comprehend, they do not possess
the freewill to disobey. Satan, on the other hand, was not an
angel. He was a Jinn created out of smokeless fire, therefore, he possessed freewill.

Question: Can angels be seen with the naked eye?

Answer: Since angels are spiritual beings, ordinary
human beings cannot see them in their natural form, unless
they take on a visible form. Prophets, on the other hand, are
bestowed with a special gift that allows them to observe
angels in their natural form. Moreover, Prophets also possess the special Allah-given ability to have conversations
with the angels. According to a narration by Aisha, may
Allah be pleased with her, recorded in *Bukhari*, the noble
Messenger has seen *Jibril* (Gabriel) twice in his natural
form. Furthermore, he has seen the Angel many times in
the appearance of a handsome young man who resembled
a Companion named *Dihya*. This is an indication that with
the permission of Allah, angels can take a visible physical
form. This is also quite evident in some Qur'anic verses
such as the one mentions the story of Prophet Ibrahim,
peace be upon him, as he was given the glad tidings of a son

---

[5] Qur'an: 2:33.

by three angels sent by Allah. These angels had also travelled to Prophet Lot, peace be upon him, to assist him.

There is also a *Hadith* recorded in Muslim which states that a man came to the noble Prophet and asked questions about *Iman* (faith) and *Ihsan* (perfect goodness). This occurred in a public audience and the man who visited the Prophet was no other than *Jibril* (Gabriel) himself.

Although, we as ordinary people may never actually see an angel in our lifetime, we constantly interact with them throughout our lives. The Noble Recorders (Kiraman Katibin) for example, are the two angels who stand by our right and left sides at all times to record our every deed and action. There are also many angels who protect and join us during our Prayers and worship. Apart from the countless number of angels who serve Allah at all times, there are four great angels that were distinguished from the rest. They are *Jibril, Mikail, Israfil* and *Azrail*. These great Angels were given unique duties by Allah. *Jibril* is the most distinguished of all angels. He is entrusted with conveying the Divine revelations to the Messengers of Allah. *Mikail* is the angel who is entrusted with the sustenance of all creatures. *Israfil* is the angel who will blow the Trumpet (*Sur*) indicating the time of the Judgment Day and *Azrail* is the angel of death who is entrusted with the duty of collecting the souls of all living creatures in the universe.

Without question, angels are truly astonishing creations of Allah. Those who contemplate and reflect on the angels of Allah will no doubt strengthen their belief in the All-Powerful and Omnipotent Allah, the Almighty Allah...

BELIEF IN DIVINE BOOKS
AND THE HOLY QUR'AN

B elief in Divine Books is the third article of the six principles of faith. Just as the All-Merciful has sent Prophets to guide mankind onto the path of the righteous, He has also blessed some of His Messengers with Divine revelations. The Divine revelations commenced to be revealed with the beginning of the human race. Some Prophets received Divine Books whilst others received pages (*Suhuf*). Pages were short revelations sufficient for smaller earlier tribal communities. According to a transmission from Abu Dharr, may Allah be pleased with him, one of the Companions of Prophet Muhammad, peace and blessings be upon him, Adam, peace be upon him, the first Prophet and servant of Allah, received 10 pages; *Shite*, peace be upon him, received 50 pages; Enoch (*Idris*), peace be upon him, received 30 pages and Abraham, peace be upon him, received 10 pages. Unfortunately, today, we do not have any copies of these Divine pages in our archives.

As the population of the human race grew drastically, they needed more comprehensive books which contained universal principles of guidance for humanity.

First of these Divine Books Torah, which was revealed to Moses, peace be upon him. It contained a set of Divine laws and principles. No Muslim can deny the original form of *Torah* because the Holy Qur'an informs believers that it was brought down as a book that contained *Nur* (Divine light) and guidance to righteousness.[6] Over the many years, *the Torah* has lost its originality and could not be preserved as it was revealed. The second of the holy books was revealed to *Dawud* (David), peace be upon him. It is called *Zabur* which meant 'The written thing'. In Christian literature, it is called 'Psalms of David'.

In the fifty-fifth verse of *Surah al-Isra*, the Almighty states:

وَلَقَدْ فَضَّلْنَا بَعْضَ النَّبِيِّنَ عَلَى بَعْضٍ وَآتَيْنَا دَاوُدَ زَبُوراً

Indeed, we have ranked some Prophets above others. We have bestowed the Zabur upon Dawud.[7]

The third of the holy books was revealed to Jesus, peace be upon him, and it is called *Injil* (the Bible). The word *Injil* means 'Glad Tidings' and just as Torah and Psalms of David, the Bible was too sent to the sons of Israel. The forty-sixth verse of *Surah al-Maedah* informs us that *Isa* was sent to confirm the authenticity of *Tawrat,* and he was blessed with *Injil,* a holy book of guidance and admonition to those who shield themselves from evil.[8]

According to Islamic sources, none of the original contents of the above books were completely preserved. There-

---

[6] Qur'an: 5:44.

[7] Qur'an: 17:55.

[8] Qur'an: 5:46.

fore, it is suggested to Muslims neither to refute nor to confirm the current contents of these books. Muslims accept the people who follow them as "the People of the Book."

The Holy Qur'an was revealed through a period of twenty-three years. It has been fourteen centuries since its revelation and the Holy Qur'an has been preserved just as it was revealed to the Prophet. According to Arabic lexicon, the definition of the word Qur'an is, 'to read, to compose or to collect'. Qur'an is the word of Allah revealed to His Messenger through Angel Gabriel (Jibril) in the form of *Wahy* (Divine revelation). The Holy Qur'an is also given the title of *Kitab Allah* which means the book of Allah. Qur'an is a book that even its recital is considered as a form of worship. Moreover, its verses are also recited during the Prescribed Prayers. The Holy Qur'an is protected by Allah himself and this is clearly stated in the Qur'an. It is a book that cannot be altered; even a modification made on a single letter will be noticed immediately by thousands of Islamic scholars and *hafiz* (people who memorize the entire Qur'an) all over the world.

The Holy Qur'an has descended from the Highest of the most High as a collection of Divine Laws containing the most perfect messages. It is the greatest honor bestowed upon humanity. The Qur'an addresses the mind, spirit, heart and the physical being of humans. As it enters the heart, it illuminates the soul, nourishes the mind and disciplines the physical body. The Qur'an teaches the meaning of existence and humanity, the truth and wisdom, as well as the essence, attributes and the meanings of the Most Beautiful Names of Allah.

It is a book that protects the innocent and cautions the tyrant. It is a book of spirituality and worship, as well as a book of social justice, fairness, freedom, equality and human rights. The Qur'an teaches humanity the secrets of worldly and eternal contentment. It shows the path to happiness and builds a bridge to the realm of eternity. It shows believers how to rise to the highest rank possible for humanity. The Qur'an facilitates a direct conversation with the Almighty Allah, the Creator and the Sustainer of the worlds.

The salvation of humanity is in the Qur'an. It is a book that brings meaning to the universe as it establishes a connection between the physical existence and its Designer. Its literature is unlike any other book or written literature. It was revealed to a person who did not know how to write or read. The Qur'anic scriptures are quite unique. They display a remarkable distinction even to the literature of the *Hadiths,* words of the Prophet. Moreover, the Qur'an brings solutions to personal, spiritual, social and even scientific issues. Fourteen hundred years after its revelation, scholars and modern academics continue to discover new signs, information and truths in the Holy Qur'an. The Holy Qur'an was the greatest miracle of the Prophet. It is the ultimate miracle bestowed upon humanity and it will continue to guide humanity until the Day of Judgment.

The matchless beauty of the Holy Qur'an is explained by Fethullah Gülen, contemporary Islamic Scholar, in his book *Pearls of Wisdom*:

> In accordance with humanity's worth and value, and considering the human heart, spirit, mind, and physical being, the Qur'an descended from the Highest of the High. Containing the most perfect messages, it is a collection of Divine Laws.
>
> Followed today by more than one billion people, the Qur'an is a unique book that, with its eternal and unchanging Divine principles, guides everyone to the shortest and most illuminated road to happiness.
>
> The Qur'an has been a source of light for the most magnificent and enlightened communities that have ruled the world, those that have produced thousands of scholars, philosophers and thinkers. In this sense, no other rule is equal to its rule.
>
> Since the day it was revealed, the Qur'an has encountered many objections and criticisms. However, the Qur'an has always emerged unscathed and so continues to reflect its victory.
>
> The Qur'an crystallizes in the heart, illumines the spirit, and exhibits truths from beginning to end. Only believers who can sense all the beauty of the universe in a single flower and see rainstorms in a drop of water can know and understand its real countenance.
>
> The Qur'an possesses such a style that Arab and foreign linguists and literary men and women who heard its verses bowed before it. Those who recognized its truth and understood its contents bowed before this masterpiece of eloquence.
>
> Muslims can reach unity only by affirming and believing the Qur'an. Those who cannot do so can-

not be Muslim, nor can they establish any lasting unity among themselves.

Saying that "faith is a matter of conscience" means "I affirm Allah, His Prophet, and the Qur'an" with my tongue and my conscience. Every act of worship connected to this understanding manifests this affirmation.

When humanity was floundering in the brutality of ignorance and unbelief, the Qur'an burst forth in a flood of enlightenment that drowned the world in its light. The Qur'an engendered a revolution without parallel or equal. History is a sufficient witness!

The Qur'an teaches in a most balanced way the meaning and nature of humanity, and the truth and wisdom, as well as the Essence, Attributes, and Names of Allah. No other book can equal it in this field. Look at the wisdom of scholarly saints and the philosophy of true philosophers, and you will understand.

The Qur'an is the unique book commanding true justice, real freedom, balanced equality, goodness, honor, virtue, and compassion for all creation. It is also the matchless book forbidding oppression, polytheism, injustice, ignorance, bribery, interest, lying, and bearing false witness.

The Qur'an is the only book that, protecting the orphan, the poor and the innocent, puts the king and the slave, the commander and the private, the plaintiff and the defendant in the same chair and then judges them.

Claiming that the Qur'an is a source of superstition is nothing more than repeating the words uttered by ignorant Arabs fourteen centuries ago. Such a view ridicules wisdom and true philosophy.

If only those who criticize the Qur'an and the things it brought could produce something to guarantee the order, harmony, peace and safety of human life even in a short, temporary period... Actually, it's very difficult to understand this perversity and obstinacy when faced with the miserable and unbalanced civilizations based on principles foreign to the Qur'an, and the troubled, depressed, and moaning hearts of those deprived of its light.

The most orderly life for humanity is that breathed by the Qur'an. In fact, some of the beautiful things that are today universally commended and applauded are the exact things encouraged by the Qur'an centuries ago. So, whose fault is it if Muslims are in a miserable situation today?

Those who criticize the Qur'an as if it were their profession generally have only a vague and superficial knowledge of its contents. It is ironic that such people feel free to vent their opinions without researching the Qur'an or even reading it. Actually, there is no difference between their attitude and the obstinacy some ignorant people show in the face of (positive) sciences. It seems that we must continue to wait for people to awaken to truth.

The Qur'an enables people to rise to the highest level, namely the station of being addressed by Allah. Those who are conscious of being in this position hear their Lord speak to them through the Qur'an. If they take an oath that they speak with their Lord, they will not be among those who swear falsely.

Even though we are still in this world, when we enter the Qur'an's enlightened climate we feel that we are passing through the grave and the intermediate world (between this and the next), experiencing the Day of Judgment and the *Sirat* (bridge), shuddering at the horror of Hell, and walking on Heaven's tranquil slopes.

Those who have prevented Muslims from understanding the Qur'an and perceiving it in depth have thus removed them from Islam's spirit and essence.

In the near future, and under humanity's gazes of commendation and amazement, the streams of knowledge, technique, and art flowing toward the Qur'anic Ocean will fall into their essential source and unite with it. At that time, scholars, researchers, and artists will find themselves in that same ocean.

It should not be too hard to see the future as the Age of the Qur'an, for it is the word of One Who sees the past, present, and future at the same moment.[9]

---

[9] Fethullah Gülen, *Pearls of Wisdom*, Light Publishing 2005.

BELIEF IN THE PROPHETS

B elief in Allah's Prophets is the fourth article of the six articles of faith. Prophethood is the highest rank that any of Allah's servants could ever reach. It is a title that cannot be attained through freewill, knowledge or effort. It is a rank granted directly by the Almighty Himself. Prophets are unique individuals whose lives are dedicated to serving the religion of Allah and humanity. They are sent to guide humanity out of the dark abysses of disbelief into the incandescent light of faith. Prophets are the fruits of compassion. Humanity has learned to embrace and implement the most basic essentials of human values and ethics through the exalted teachings of the Prophets.

Prophets arrive with answers to most intricate philosophical and scientific questions generated by the human mind, such as, *"who am I? Where do I come from? What is my purpose on earth and where am I going?"*

Prophets deliver an elixir which brings hope, tranquility, peace and contentment to the heart. And they bring principles that establish order, harmony, understanding, justice and compassion among human beings. It is through them, we discover the secrets of eternity and immortality.

Without Prophets, past would be regarded as an immense grave that has swollen every living creature on its path and the future would be considered as the inevitable end that waits impatiently to annihilate all forms of life in the universe. Therefore, the luminous torch carried by the Prophets sheds a light into the dark past and onto the unknown future.

Throughout history, human tribes and nations have never been deprived of Prophets. Beginning with Adam, peace be upon him, the All-Compassionate has sent thousands of Prophets who guided humanity onto the right path. It was Noah, peace be upon him, who battled colossal waves to deliver a handful of believers to the safety of Mt Judi. It was Abraham, peace be upon him, who had to be cast into a blazing inferno in order to deliver his sanctified message. Jonah, peace be upon him, struggled in the belly of a giant fish and Moses, peace be upon him, wondered through the dry desert for many months as he starved and suffered for his noble cause. David, peace be upon him, had to confront Goliath and Jesus, peace be upon him, endured the pain of torture and harassment.

In the Holy Qur'an, Allah the Almighty informs us that He has sent a Messenger to all human clans and nations:

اِنَّا اَرْسَلْنَاكَ بِالْحَقِّ بَشِيراً وَنَذِيراً وَاِنْ مِنْ اُمَّةٍ اِلَّا خَلَا فِيهَا نَذِيرٌ

Verily! We have sent you with the truth, a bearer of glad tidings, and a warner. And there never was a nation but a warner had passed among them.[10]

وَلَقَدْ بَعَثْنَا فِى كُلِّ أُمَّةٍ رَسُولاً

And verily, We have sent among every community, nation a Messenger...[11]

It is quite clear that Allah has sent a Messenger to all nations and tribes so that they would be guided onto the right path. Historically, whenever mankind inclined towards evil and rebellion, they were blessed with a Prophet who came to them with a sacred message from Allah. The Holy Qur'an mentions the names of twenty-five most significant Prophets.

Prophets mentioned in the Qur'an are listed below with their Arabic and English names:

1. Adam - Adam
2. Idris - Enoch
3. Nuh - Noah
4. Hud
5. Saleh
6. Ibrahim - Abraham
7. Lut - Lot
8. Ismail - Ishmael
9. Ishaq - Isaac
10. Yaqub - Jacob

---

[10] Qur'an: 35:24.
[11] Qur'an: 16:36.

11. Yusuf - Joseph
12. Ayyub - Job
13. Shuayb - Jethro
14. Musa - Moses
15. Harun - Aaron
16. Dhul-Kifl - Ezekiel
17. Dawud - David
18. Suleyman - Solomon
19. Ilyas - Elijah
20. Al-Yasa - Elisha
21. Yunus - Jonah
22. Zakariya - Zachary
23. Yahya - John the Baptist
24. Isa - Jesus
25. Muhammad (peace and blessings be upon them all)

However, according to a *hadith*, sayings of the Last Prophet, Allah has sent approximately 124,000 Prophets to humanity since the beginning of history.

The Emergence of the Last Prophet

Pre-Islamic Arabia was dominated by superstitions, barbarous and violent customs, and degraded moral standards. Feeling disgraced and ashamed, fathers would bury their daughters alive. Children of the poor who could not pay their debts, would be taken away to be enslaved and sold in the slave markets. Tribe members would slay each other over the simplest of issues and the women of this society were classified as second grade human beings. Human life had no value and there was no justice system to protect the innocent. Out of various materials, people would make idols and worship them as gods.

The people of wisdom and righteousness were looking for a light that could brighten their world and liberate their society from this repugnant way of life. The coming of the light of salvation mentioned in the previous scriptures was impatiently awaited by a handful of righteous people who believed in the Lord of Ibrahim, peace be upon him. They also lived amongst this tribal society but denounced all forms of idol worshipping and the wicked ways of the polytheists. They knew that their Lord would soon send a savior. According to previous scriptures the awaited one would be Allah's last Messenger on earth.

A rose most unique and magnificent had already bloomed in the middle of the desert forty years prior to the night which would change the destiny of humanity. The prayers of the righteous were answered and on the night of *Qadr*, 610 CE, Allah blessed humanity with His last Messenger. Suddenly, a dark cave on *Mt Nur* began to glow with an inexplicable radiance. Archangel *Jibril* who had visited all previous Messengers of Allah had appeared before Muhammad, peace and blessings be upon him, in all of his glory and majesty. "Read", the angel said to Muhammad, peace and blessings be upon him, who did not know how to read. He replied, "I cannot". The angel then repeated, "Read in the name of your Lord". Miraculously, Muhammad, peace and blessings be upon him, began to read. These were the first verses revealed from the Holy Qur'an. An orphan from the tribe of *Quraysh* was given the noblest of all duties. He was the last Messenger of Allah. Through him, Allah would complete His religion.

The Messenger of Allah was unique in all aspects. The matchless qualities of all the previous Prophets were congregated in him. On the day he was born, he had cried out "my community… my community." Throughout his sanctified life, he uttered the very same words and on the day he passed away, he left in the same manner as he repeated the words, "my community… my community."

The Prophet was so unique that the Almighty had blessed him the title of *Habib-Allah* which meant the beloved of Allah. Furthermore, people of his era, those who believed him and those who did not, gave him the title of *al-Amin* which meant the trustworthy. He was a man who emitted trust and a sense of tranquility to all those around him. The last Messenger of Allah was so different that there were occasions where the most stubborn idol-worshippers embraced his faith by just taking a glimpse of his luminous face. Once he had declared his mission of prophethood to a tribal chief. Following a brief gaze of the Prophet's noble face, the man replied, "There is no lie on this face".

The noble Messenger came with a key that unlocked the mysteries of the universe. He explained the purpose of life and the meaning of existence. Through him, humanity learned what awaited them beyond the grave. He cleared all forms of ambiguity and haziness from the minds of confused human beings. He brought hope and exuberance into the lives of those in despair and desolation.

It was the noble Messenger who showed humanity ways to satisfy the heart and the soul. These were the two entities that could only be satisfied with the love and remembrance of Allah. Following the arrival of the noble Prophet, life began to take on a new meaning. Heads began to bow before the Almighty Allah and hearts submitted to Him with absolute obedience. He taught believers how to believe, submit and how to practice the religion of Allah. He preached love, compassion, understanding, mutual respect, harmony, fairness, charity and empathy for all of Allah's creatures. He practiced whatever he preached with utmost sensitivity and more than anyone ever could.

It was through him that humanity learned to worship the one and only Allah and to respect their elders and fellow human beings. And it was his teachings that taught people to refrain from stealing, cheating, lying and deceiving each other. He encouraged the wealthy to help the poor, needy, orphan and the widower. He showed believers how to pray, fast, perform the holy pilgrimage and to give charity. He showed people how to live and die like true human beings. And he taught his followers how to please Allah as he guided them to the path that led to the eternal paradise. The noble Messenger of Allah turned an ignorant barbaric tribal community into a noble society that established the foundations of modern civilization. It had taken him a mere twenty-three years to accomplish such an astonishing change that encompassed spiritual, personal, social and political rejuvenation.

The Qur'an astounded the Arabs of his era and continues to amaze people of sound understanding. Moreover, no book of similar articulateness has ever been produced to this day. The Holy Qur'an has also been read and memorized for over fourteen-hundred years by millions of non-Arabs, even those who do not understand or speak Arabic find pleasure in reading it.

The Prophet's Departure from This World

The Messenger of Allah lived a life of struggle. From the age of forty to the age of six-three, he conveyed the message of Allah to humanity and dedicated his life to serving Allah and establishing the foundations of a pious, righteous, harmonious and just society that would be the benchmark for all future generations. He was the beloved servant of Allah, a man loved passionately by his followers and respected even by his enemies.

Following a short twenty-three years of Prophethood, in which he managed to squeeze accomplishments of a grandeur nature that could only be achieved in a thousand years, the noble Messenger of Allah completed his mission at the age of sixty-three. As his mission had been fulfilled, for him, the worldly life had lost its meaning. There was no reason for him to remain on earth any longer.

The time of departure had arrived. He had come to a stage where Prayers were the only thing that attached him to this life. He was sixty-three and calendars were displaying the 8th of June 632 CE. The noble Messenger became so ill that the high fever had rendered him unconscious. Each time he regained consciousness, he uttered the following words with great concern on his face, "The Prayer!" His beloved Companions replied, "The Prayer time has not entered yet, oh noble Messenger of Allah". Many times they had poured buckets of cold water over his noble head. His body temperature was at critical levels. Finally, the time for the Prayer had arrived. They helped him to stand up and two of his Companions supported him with their shoulders as he walked towards the mosque. The noble Messenger had no energy left in his sanctified body as he dragged his feet towards the mosque. Companions who were waiting in the mosque with tears in their eyes saw a glimmer of hope as they observed the Prophet's approach. He could not lead the Prayers anymore. It was for the first time that the noble Messenger asked Abu Bakr, may Allah be pleased with him, to lead the Prayer in his presence. This was also an indication that his beloved friend Abu Bakr was being prepared for the great job ahead.

This would be the last Prayer that the noble Messenger performed. At the conclusion of the Prayer, he returned to his blessed quarters. He asked his beloved daughter, Fatima, may Allah be pleased with her, to come close. She leaned over and placed her ear next to her father's mouth. The noble Messenger whispered some words into her ear. Fatima began to weep desperately. Once again, the Prophet asked her to approach. This time, upon hearing the words of her father, Fatima began to smile. They asked her why she had behaved this way. She replied, "On the first occasion he said, "Do not worry my daughter, from this day on your father will never feel pain again". This is when I began to weep. And then he said, "You will be the first one from my household to join me." This is when I smiled".

The time of departure had arrived, and angel of death *Azrail* requested permission from the noble Messenger to enter his quarters. The permission was granted. The angel said, "O Muhammad! I was sent by your Lord who gives you the option to live for as long as you wish". The noble Messenger replied, "Take me to the Highest Abode." The noble Prophet then departed from this world. As followers of the noble Messenger we say: "Oh the noble Prophet of Allah! Do not deprive us of your blessed intercession on the Day of Judgment!

The Noble Prophet's Achievements in 23 Years

- He established a new religion, which brought *Tawhid*, Oneness and Unity of Allah, hence abolished polytheism in Arabian Peninsula.
- He established a new way of life, implementing new laws, which eradicated the violent customs that originated from tribalism. This changed societies' perspective and brought a new order through faith and spirituality.
- He brought the Qur'an and applied his *Sunnah*. After him, both became a source of guidance for humanity.

- During his time, he established brotherhood between many Arab tribes. Later, the notion of this brotherhood spread to many other nations.
- Through faith and persuasion, he abolished or modified many unethical customs observed by the nomadic society of the region.
- Combated racism and bigotry in Arabian Peninsula by emphasizing the equality of people in the eyes of Allah.
- He established a civilized state governed by laws.
- He was the inspiration behind the formation of twenty states and empires including Andalusia, Abbasids, Umayyad's, Seljuk's, and the Ottoman Empire.

The Prophet's Farewell Sermon

O People, listen well to my words, for I do not know whether, after this year, I shall ever be amongst you again. Therefore listen to what I am saying to you very carefully and take these words to those who could not be present here today.

O People, just as you regard this month, this day, and this city as sacred, so regard the life and property of every Muslim as a sacred trust. Return the goods entrusted to you to their rightful owners. Treat others justly so that no one would be unjust to you. Remember that you will indeed meet your Lord, and that He will indeed reckon your deeds. Allah has forbidden you to take *riba,* usury; therefore all usury obligations shall henceforth be waived. Your capital, however, is yours to keep. You will neither inflict nor suffer inequity. Allah has judged that there shall be no usury and that all the usury due to Abbas ibn Abdul-muttalib, may Allah be pleased with him, shall henceforth be waived.

Every right arising out of homicide in pre-Islamic days is henceforth waived and the first such right that I waive is that arising from the murder of Rabi'ah ibn al-Harith ibn Abdulmuttalib, may Allah be pleased with him.

O Men, the nonbelievers indulge in tampering with the calendar in order to make permissible that which Allah forbade, and to forbid that which Allah has made permissible. With Allah the months are twelve in number. Four of them are sacred, three of these are successive and one occurs singly between the months of Jumada and Sha'ban. Beware of Satan, for the safety of your religion. He has lost all hope that he will ever be able to lead you astray in big things, so beware of following him in small things.

O People, it is true that you have certain rights over your women, but they also have rights over you. Remember that you have taken them as your wives only under Allah's trust and with His permission. If they abide by your right then to them belongs the right to be fed and clothed in kindness. Treat your women well and be kind to them, for they are your partners and committed helpers. It is your right and they do not make friends with anyone of whom you do not approve, as well as never to be unchaste...

O People listen to me in earnest, worship Allah (The One and only Creator of the universe), perform your five Daily Prayers, *Salah*, fast during the month of Ramadan, and give your financial obligation, *Zakah*, of your wealth. Perform *Hajj*, the holy pilgrimage if you can afford to.

All mankind is from Adam and Eve, an Arab has no superiority over a non-Arab nor a non-Arab has any superiority over an Arab; also a white has no superiority over a black nor does a black have any superiority over white except by piety and good action. Learn that every Muslim is a brother to every Muslim and that all Muslims constitute one brotherhood. Nothing shall be legitimate to a Muslim which belongs to a fellow Muslim unless it was given freely and willingly. Do not, therefore, do injustice to yourselves. Remember, one day you will appear before Allah and you will answer for your deeds. So beware, do not stray from the path of righteousness after I am gone.

O People, no Prophet or Messenger will come after me and no new faith will be born. Reason well, therefore, O People, and understand words which I convey to you. I am leaving you with the Book of Allah, the Holy Qur'an and my *Sunnah;* if you follow them you will never go astray.

All those who listen to me shall pass on my words to others and those to others again; and may the last ones understand my words better than those who listen to me directly. Be my witness O Lord, I have conveyed your message to your people.

BELIEF IN LIFE AFTER DEATH

B elief in life after death is one of the most important articles of faith. It is having faith in the hereafter that gives humanity hope and strength to
endure the burdens of worldly life. Life after death is an
answer to the deepest prayers of the human soul. Resurrection and eternal life is a promise given to humankind by
the Almighty Himself, therefore, its existence cannot be
questioned. The Divine Names of Allah necessitate the
existence of a realm of justice, reward and punishment.

Without Judgment Day and life after death, this world
would transform into a realm of injustice, tyranny, disap-
pointment and delusion. Those who have not been apprehended for their crimes on earth could not be punished
and those who live a life of piety and righteousness could
not be rewarded. It is an obvious fact that true justice can
never be achieved on earth. We live in a world where some
indulge themselves in the pleasures of wealth and prosperity whilst others battle with starvation as they struggle to
find a morsel of food. The human justice system does not
always favor the truth as it operates with ambiguities and
loopholes. Since Allah is Just, this alone requires the establishment of a Day of Judgment where everyone is dealt

with fairly. Without doubt, Allah hears the desperate screams of millions of people who cry out for justice.

There is also the reality that pleasure and pain are intermingled in this life hence true pleasure can never be experienced in the presence of pain. Statistically, on average a human being experiences six months of pleasure in his/her life. According to a research, we spend 25 years of our lives sleeping. Eight hours of sleep a day means one third of our daily lives, therefore, an individual who lives to the age of 75 has spend 25 years of his/her life sleeping. When we remove activities such as education, work, daily choirs, illnesses, dealing with problems, bath and toilet time, and the burdens of old age from the remaining 50 years, we are left with no more than six months of pleasure. The results of this research clearly state that the world we live in is not a realm of gratification, entertainment or games, but a world of testing and assessment. Moreover, there are many who do not even live long enough to experience adulthood. There are also those who suffer throughout their lives, struggling with poverty, sickness and oppression. Considering all of the above, without the establishment of a hereafter, this temporary life would contradict the Mercy, Compassion and Justice of Allah.

Let us illuminate the issue with an analogy:

Imagine a generous King who invites the entire inhabitants of a poor village to his palace. All the guests arrive to the King's palace where they are welcomed with a magnificent feast and entertainment. They enjoy and indulge themselves for 75 hours in the King's palace. During the program the King distributes bags of gold coins to his servants. Everyone is happy and full of bliss. At the conclusion of the program, the guests are taken out of the palace one by one and hanged in the garden.

Now, can any person of logic claim that the King is a compassionate, merciful and a generous ruler? On the contrary, he would be a merciless tyrant who gave his servants a sample of his wealth and bounties and then condemned them to death.

Just as in the analogy above, human beings are transitory guests in this great palace we call earth. Like the villagers who enjoyed 75 hours of pleasure in the palace, we enjoy 75 years of life on this planet. We benefit from the bounties and pleasures of this world until such a time that death takes everything away from us. However, unlike the story above, the King of this world is not a tyrant. On the contrary, He is the All-Compassionate, the All-Merciful, the All-Munificent and the All-Generous Allah. His treasures are limitless. His power has no boundaries. His existence is eternal in the past and everlasting in the future. He has created human beings so that they would recognize His Might, observe His magnificent art and benefit from His Mercy and Compassion. Therefore, eternal power necessitates eternal observers; eternal Mercy and Compassion necessitates eternal beneficiaries; eternal wealth necessitates eternal recipients; eternal Munificence necessitates eternal gratefulness and Exalted Justice necessitates the establishment of a realm where everyone is dealt with fairly. Accordingly, all human beings will certainly be resurrected and held accountable for their lives spent on this transient world of assessment. Consequently, they will either be rewarded for their good deeds or punished for their evil.

Although, there are countless proofs and evidences to the establishment of a life after death, the Holy Qur'an and the presence of the noble Messenger of Allah is the greatest evidence to the hereafter. Along with these two unquestionable authentic proofs there are other solid evidences such as the previous Divine Books, Prophets and thousands of saints and scholars who all claimed the very same thing: "There is life after death." Moreover, history verifies that all of these individuals who make the very same claim has never lied or even exaggerated in their lives.

Question: Since one-fifth of the Holy Qur'an talks about the life after death and the noble Messenger have informed us about the Day of Judgment, we have no reservations about its existence. However, some people find it difficult to comprehend the concept of resurrection and a life after death. What can we say to them?

Answer: Obviously, it is difficult to comprehend a life that we have not seen or experienced, however, some evidences of a life after death can be physically observed in this life. For example; imagine a baby still in his/her mother's womb. Just for arguments sake, let us say, we had the opportunity to establish a conversation with this baby. Assuming that the baby also possesses the ability to understand us, we tell him/her about the reality of this world. We explain to him/her that the world he/she is currently in is a temporary abode from where he/she will soon come out to a bigger and larger world. We describe to him/her things that exist in this world, such as the sun, the moon, trees, ocean, rivers, flowers, millions of different life forms. Furthermore, let us say that we talk to him/her about jets, cars, trains, ships and technology. Could he/she have any concept or even imagine such things? The only world he/she has experienced for the past nine months is the tiny space in the womb hence for him/her no other world exists. The world to which he/she would soon be arriving is incomprehensible.

Human beings who were created for eternity and a realm of everlasting life are no different to a baby in the womb. In comparison to the life after, this world is like the mother's womb. Hence, imagining a world of eternity seems a difficult task for us. However, just as the baby realizes the existence of this world upon his/her birth, we will realize the existence of the hereafter upon our death. Furthermore, there are many signs and indications that the intellect can detect even in this life.

Question: So what are the signs and indications?

Answer: Once again, the answer lies in the baby allegory. During his/her time in the mother's womb the baby feeds through the umbilical cord, therefore, does not need a mouth. Also, the baby does not need eyes, ears, hands and feet in the womb, because he/she has no use for them. If the baby had the necessary intelligence to think and ponder, he/she would use his/her logic and contemplate: "Why do I possess eyes when it is dark in here? Why do I have feet when I cannot walk? Why do I have a mouth when I am being fed through my stomach?" This line of questioning will lead to the reality that the baby will indeed have use for all of the organs mentioned above, but in some other realm for which he/she is being prepared. This is quite a valid argument, because everything Allah has created comes with a corresponding counterpart or an opposite. For example, the creation of nose indicates to scent; the creation of ears indicates to sound; the creation of eyes indicates to light and so on...

However, there are some things in this life for which we fail to find a counterpart. For example, we all want to live forever, we all want everlasting wealth and health; we all want eternal youth and prosperity. Unfortunately, none of these properties exists here. But according to the reality above, Allah creates everything with a corresponding item. A famous scholar once said, *"If He did not want to give, He would not have given the feeling of want."* Since these sensations, feelings, wishes and desires of eternity exist in all human beings; their counterparts will also be created. Consequently, Allah wanted to give hence He has created the feeling of want.

Another significant point about resurrection is Allah the Almighty exhibits samples of resurrection before our very eyes each year during spring time. All trees and plant life that transform into mere logs and dried out strands comes back to life during spring, blossoming with exquisitely colorful flowers and fruits. Moreover, indication of resurrection is also manifested to us through the seeds of plants which evidently die out and decompose upon entering the dark soil of the earth. Yet, their death gives birth to a brand new life. Giving life to inanimate matter is one of Allah's Attributes. We observe this everyday in nature. By the will of Allah, life emerges from non-living matter such as carbon atoms, amino acids, nucleic acids and proteins. As mentioned previously, the notion of easy and difficult does not apply to Allah, however, for arguments sake, we would like to point out that creating something out of nothing and for the first time would plausibly be considered as more difficult than reproducing it.

Let us explain this with another allegory: Imagine an electronics wizard who walks into a room packed with a large audience, carrying a bag filled with thousands of tiny electronic components. He then opens the bag and within minutes, he puts the tiny components together and constructs a network of computer systems. He then, pulls everything apart, dismantling the entire system into tiny pieces. Can anyone in the room argue that this person is incapable of putting the same system together again and making it work? Certainly not! Simply because he has already proven that he has the ability and capability to construct and built extremely complex systems.

An existing product points to its maker and it is the greatest evidence that the maker has the talent and the power to reproduce it.

The allegory above is closely related to an incident which took place during the time of the noble Messenger of Allah. A man came up to the noble Prophet holding a

chinbone of a dead camel in his hand. He asked with sar-
casm, "Who will give life to this"? The Holy Qur'an
answered his question with a verse from Surah Yasin:

وَضَرَبَ لَنَا مَثَلاً وَنَسِيَ خَلْقَهُ قَالَ مَنْ يُحْيِ الْعِظَامَ وَهِيَ رَمِيمٌ

*And he makes comparisons for Us, and forgets his own
(origin and) Creation: He says, "Who can give life to
(dry) bones and decomposed ones (at that)?*[12]

The Holy Qur'an provides the most perfect answer to
those who doubt resurrection. Do they not look at their
own origin? Indeed, those who doubt resurrection should
look at the origin of all life forms on earth and the origin
of the universe. It is the Omnipotent Allah, the Almighty
Allah who created the universe and the life forms that
dwell in it. He then, exhibited His grand art to those who
has the ability to think and comprehend. Obviously, creating everything and giving life to the dead is within the
limits of His Power and Wisdom. Just as a general who
reassembles an entire army which had taken a rest break,
with one commandment, the All-Powerful will too bring
together the decomposed components of all human beings
who had died and resurrect them on the promised Day of
Judgment.

The Holy Qur'an instructs us to scrutinize our own origin. Although, there have been many scientific theories and
proposal regarding the origin of life on earth, no scientist or
thinker has provided answers to the metaphysical link

---

[12] Qur'an: 36:78.

between non-living matter and living organisms. How does non-living matter transform into a living organism? What is life and where does it come from? To make things more complex, there are no valid scientific arguments for the origin of the universe and the entire existence. Fritz Schaefer, the Graham Perdue Professor of Chemistry and the Director of the Center for Computational Quantum Chemistry at the University of Georgia, makes the following points regarding the creation of the universe:

1. **The cosmological argument:** the effect of the universe's existence must have a suitable cause.
2. **The teleological argument:** the design of the universe implies a purpose or direction behind it.
3. **The rational argument:** the operation of the universe, according to order and natural law, implies a mind behind it.[13]

The scientific and philosophical arguments clearly indicate that the entire existence, including life is a product of a magnificent creation. There is a point in the research regarding the origin of matter where science fails to provide any answers. It is at this point many physicists choose to invoke Allah by proposing that the universe had to be created. Creation necessitates a Creator hence it is also palpable that He who creates out of nothing, certainly possesses the power to recreate or reproduce. Consequently, Allah will most certainly resurrect humanity and establish the Day of Judgment just as He promises in the Holy Qur'an.

---

[13] U.S. News & World Report, Dec. 23, 1991.

BELIEF IN DESTINY

Belief in destiny is the sixth principle of the six articles of faith. Belief in destiny is an obligatory principle for all Muslims. One's faith cannot be complete without belief in destiny. However, destiny is one of the most controversial topics of faith. The notion of destiny and fate has always been a most confusing concept for both believers and nonbelievers alike. Some scholars have even suggested that it is a profound matter that should not be meddled around with so extensively. Conversely, in order to possess a strong faith, one needs to satisfy both his/her heart and intellect. Therefore, we will attempt to shed light onto some perplexing issues of destiny.

Understanding destiny runs parallel to understanding the concept of space-time. Space and time are created entities that co-exist. Moreover, they exist simultaneously, which means the past, present and the future with their corresponding space exists at the same instant. However, all of Allah's creatures are trapped within their own space-time. In simple terms, for us, the past is past and the future has not arrived yet. Yet, for Allah, they all exist at the very same time. The reason for this is; Allah is not restricted by space or time. They are all His creations; therefore He has the power and knowledge to observe the past, present and future altogether.

According to Islamic teachings, Allah has recorded everything that occurred in the past, present and that will occur in the future. The space-time explanation above authenticates that this is quite easy for Him since He observes everything simultaneously. He has knowledge of all that occurs at the same instant. The concept of easy-difficult does not apply to Allah, but we have used it here so that the issue could be comprehended with simplicity. According to Islamic teachings, everything that has occurred, is occurring and will occur is recorded in a book titled *Kitabul Qadar,* the book of destiny. This means whatever occurs in the entire universe, including everything that occurs throughout the lives of all human beings is recorded in this book. Even the exact amount of breaths that a person will take and the number of times his/her heart will beat throughout his/her life is recorded in this Divine book of destiny.

Question: If Allah has prewritten everyone's destiny then is it just to hold someone accountable for his crimes or rebellion when he had no other option but to fulfill his destiny?

Answer: Yes, it is just and fair because the offender has made the decision using his/her own freewill. In order to illuminate this, we should take a look at the following analogy:

Let us assume that a scientist has developed the technology to look into the future and he has decided to

browse into the future of his neighbor. Using his equip-
ment, he observes everything that his neighbor will do
within the next 24 hours. During his observations he realizes that ten hours into his future, the neighbor will commit a serious crime. The scientist records everything he
observes. His observations become a reality and the neighbor is apprehended for the crime.

According to this metaphor, can the offender blame the
scientist for the crime he has committed by claiming that
he had already recorded his actions prior to the crime
being committed and therefore he had written and decided his destiny, when he faces court and punishment? Certainly not, because the offender acted on his own freewill.
Therefore, the scientist cannot be held accountable for his
prior knowledge of the events that would eventually take
place. Consequently, having prior knowledge of something is not the same as enforcing it.

In order to grasp a better understanding of destiny and
freewill, one must first comprehend the meaning of the
following principle:

**'Knowledge depends on the evident (actuality) but
the evident does not depend on knowledge.'** For example, our local newspapers inform us about the exact time
that the sun will rise the next day. This information provided to us is knowledge. The rising of the sun at that
given time is the evident. The rising of the sun does not
depend on the information provided to us by the newspapers but the information given to us by the newspapers
depends on the actual time of the sunrise. What this

means is the sun would have risen at that particular time, whether the information was available or not. Yet, the information provided to us by the observatories can be considered as the sun's destiny. Similarly, with His infinite knowledge, Allah knows everything that will occur in the future therefore, He has recorded everything that would occur in His Divine book of destiny. There is however, a slight distinction: not only does Allah possess information about the future, but He also creates it.

Question: How could destiny and freewill co-exist?

Answer: Destiny exists so that human beings do not ascribe success and accomplishments to themselves; freewill exists so that human beings do not refuse responsibility for their actions and deeds. For example, it is Allah Who grants various talents to human beings; however, it is freewill that encourages human beings to develop and improve their given talents. Being a champion athlete requires hard work but the potential to become a champion was granted by Allah. This means that Allah creates human beings with the potential to do good or evil. However, the choice is left to the individual. It is freewill that enables us to improve ourselves yet the process of improvement is created by Allah. In a sense, we could say that we make the intention and Allah creates the action.

Question: Does this mean that we can change our destiny?

Answer: The answer to this question is yes and no. Let us explain this with an example from the time of the Companions of the Prophet:

It was during the caliphate of Umar ibn al-Khattab. One day, Umar decided to travel to Damascus with a group of men. Along the way, a man coming from the direction of Damascus brought a message. He warned them of a plague epidemic in the city. Umar then consulted his men and decided to return to Medina. One of the men in his group stood up and said, "Shame on you, O Umar! Are you running from the destiny of Allah?" Umar replied, as he pointed towards Damascus and then towards Medina, "It is you who should be ashamed. You did not understand the concept of destiny. Indeed, I am running from the destiny of Allah, to the destiny of Allah." The incident teaches us that it is our duty to abide by the laws of physics and nature. However, the result is created by Allah. Therefore, whatever happens as a result must be considered as the destiny of Allah.

This means, changing our decisions in life does not change the information which Allah has recorded in the book of destiny. The reason for this is Allah can see our future at the same time as He sees our present. Therefore, He already knows what our choices will be.

Let us complete the issue with a comprehensive analogy:

Imagine that the book you are currently holding in your hand contains the entire existence from the beginning of time until the end. For instance, the first page of the book represents the creation of the universe and last page signifies the end of the universe. Let us say that the current page you are reading is the universe at its current stage and time.

Everything that exists—including all human beings living on this planet now—is trapped in the current page you are reading. Therefore, we cannot go to the previous pages nor can we move to the following pages. Our destiny lies in the following pages yet we have no knowledge of it. However, Allah the Almighty observes all pages at the same instant and simultaneously. Therefore, He knows all that will occur, hence He has recorded all. However, His knowledge of our destiny does not remove our responsibility of being virtuous human beings. For everything we commit and every act we perform in the future, we will use our freewill and therefore we will be held accountable.

There is another important point that one should never forget; Allah is the Creator of all that exists, including the future. This means that using freewill to decide on a certain act does not mean accomplishing it. The human potency does not go beyond a mere decision. It is Allah who creates our wishes if He wills. Consequently, we decide and He creates, if He wills. We make the intention and the attempt but we cannot interfere in the result. Evidently, we are not the creators of even our own actions. Our responsibility lies in our intentions and decisions. It is Allah who creates everything and anything.

Question: Does this mean that Allah also creates evil?

Answer: The creation of evil is not evil but the acting of evil is evil. What this means is Allah creates certain properties so that they may serve many beneficial purposes. However, some of His creation can also be used for evil. For example, Allah created fire so that we can use it for light, heat energy and so on. However, if a person casts another person into a blazing fire, would he have the right to claim that Allah has created an evil like fire? The creation of fire is not evil but using it for an evil purpose is evil. Moreover, sometimes incidents that seem as evil to us may in fact conceal a Divine purpose. Since we do not possess the power to look into the future or on some occasions we fail to see the bigger picture, we can interpret certain occurrences as evil, even though they may have occurred for a Divine purpose or for a blessed cause.

It is our duty as human beings to obey the laws of nature which were created by Allah. However, we need to also understand that results are created by Allah. For example, if we are ill, we need to seek remedy or cure for our illness. However, we should also acknowledge that our recovery depends on Allah's decision. An important Islamic scholar explains that submission to Allah's will does not mean giving up on causes. True submission is achieved through precaution and obedience to the causes which were created by Allah.

Once, a Companion of the noble Prophet came to the mosque riding a camel. He dismounted his camel and asked the Prophet, "Should I tie him up or should I submit to Allah's will?" The noble Messenger of Allah replied, "Secure your camel and then submit to the will of Allah." It is quite clear that human beings need to use their free-will and the causes provided to them in order to accomplish what is best in life. However, results need to be left to Allah and should never be questioned after they occur.

Belief in destiny is also a great remedy for some psychological disorders such as depression, fear of future and anxiety. Being assured of the fact that our future is in the hands of Allah the Almighty, provides a certain sense of tranquility and serenity in the mind and heart.

The statement of a great historical commander is the best example for this. Jalaladdin Khwarazm-Shah was a commander who had never lost a battle. One day, as he prepared for another battle, one of his viziers came to him and said, "O sire, today you will be victorious again!" The great commander replied, "I shall go into battle all prepared because this is my duty. However, victory belongs to Allah. It is He who will decide on whether we win or lose!"

This means that using their freewill, human beings need to show the effort to succeed in life but should never interfere in Allah's decision because the result is His destiny. It is this concept of destiny that enables human beings to endure the pains and sufferings of life whilst it provides hope and optimism about the future.

Final word: destiny and freewill are the two realities that co-exist. It is destiny that prevents human beings from developing pharaoh-like egos and arrogance. And, it is freewill that protects human beings from refusing or denying responsibility or accountability for their actions.

FIVE PILLARS OF ISLAM

THE TESTIMONY OF FAITH

The testimony of faith is the first pillar of Islam. In Islamic terminology, the testimony or declaration of faith is called the *Shahadah* and it is the decisive criterion by which a human being is judged to be a Muslim or a nonbeliever. This testimony is the very foundation upon which Islam is based. By reciting the *Shahadah* a believer declares "I bear witness that there is no deity but Allah and I bear witness that Muhammad is His servant and Messenger". There are three important components to this testimony:

First: The testimony of faith denies all false gods and idols. Other than Allah, it rejects everything that is worshipped, including worldly temptations.

Second: The testimony of faith verifies and limits divinity to Almighty Allah alone. That is, the servant must believe and affirm Allah is the true and One and only Allah, and offer accordingly no act of worship to anyone or anything else other than Allah.

Third: The second component of the testimony of faith establishes that the believer acknowledges the prophethood of Muhammad by declaring that he is the servant and Messenger of Allah whom the Holy Qur'an was revealed.

THE PRESCRIBED PRAYERS

قَدْ اَفْلَحَ الْمُؤْمِنُونَ ۞ الَّذِينَ هُمْ فِى صَلَاتِهِمْ خَاشِعُونَ

Prosperous indeed are the believers. Those who humble themselves in their Prayers.[14]

The second pillar of Islam is *Salah* (Prescribed Prayers). After faith, the Prescribed Prayers are the greatest reality in the universe. *Salah* is a complete form of worship that establishes a direct connection between the believer and the Almighty Allah. *Salah* is a display of one's weakness and impotence before the All-Powerful Allah. It is also a type of declaration made by the worshipper in recognition of the Might of Allah. No other form of worship brings human beings closer to Allah than *Salah*.

As the believer goes to the prostration position in total humility, he/she is aware of the fact that there is no intermediary between him/her and the All-Merciful. This is the exact point where the believer can open his/her heart fully to his/her Lord in total submission and capitulation. During *Sajdah,* the prostration position, the believer realizes he/she is before the Lord of the universes, the Almighty

---

[14] Qur'an: 23:1–2.

Allah, the All-Merciful and the All-Forgiving. The worshipper is also in complete comprehension of the reality that nothing can come between them.

Through *Salah,* the observer declares that he/she worships Allah only and he/she seeks only His help. *Salah* is also a statement that proclaims "This head bows before no one but you O Lord!" This means that the worshipper does not bow down before worldly wealth, possessions or ranks. He/she does not give into temptations of the flesh or the carnal animalistic desires.

Salah is one of the five pillars of Islam but within it contains all the other pillars. The first pillar of Islam is the testimony of faith and this is recited in *Salah.* The second pillar of Islam is *Salah* itself. The third pillar of Islam is the Ramadan fast and during *Salah,* one must abstain from eating, drinking and all kinds of acts that break the fast. The fourth pillar of Islam is the holy pilgrimage and during *Salah* the performer faces *Ka'ba* hence, in a sense performs Hajj, the holy pilgrimage. The fifth pillar of Islam is *Zakah*, the compulsory alms-giving and during *Salah*, the worshipper gives alms from his physical health and being through bodily motions performed in the Prayer.

All roads that lead to the eternal contentment pass through *Salah*. During *Salah*, humans transform into angelic beings. From the moment hands are raised and the *Takbir* "Allah is the greatest" is recited, the worshiper cuts all ties with the physical universe. The worshipper enters into a metaphysical realm where matter has no meaning. He/she is standing before the Creator of all existence. As the worshipper becomes two-fold before his/her Lord, he/she enters into a new phase of submission. At *Ruku*, the observer fixes his/her eyes on the position of *Sajdah*, the place of prostration. By now, his/her heart, soul and body become exceptionally impatient. All of his/her faculties are longing for *Sajdah*, because it is the point where true proximity with Allah is achieved. Once the head goes to the prostration position, the worshipper is not of this world anymore. Although, physically the worshipper remains in this world, spiritually he/she is by the side of his/her Lord.

Indeed, prostration position is regarded as proximity to the doors of Mercy where the worshipper waits to be accepted... At this point, the observer's heart is beating like a drum as the level of excitement increases each time he/she utters the words, *Subhana Rabbi al a'la,* Glory be to my Lord, the Most High. This is a stage where the worshipper is in total suspense as he/she ponders, "what if the doors of Mercy open and I am welcomed?" This is when absolute tranquility and serenity sets in. The spiritual ecstasy experienced during *Sajdah* cannot be felt anywhere else.

A Muslim lives his entire life in this fashion, continuously knocking on the doors of Mercy. The knocking is accomplished through *Salah*. Can one expect a door to be opened when one does not knock? This is why the five Daily Prayers are so important in Islam. They are the keys to the doors of Mercy. On the Day of Judgment, the first thing that the servant will be held accountable for is *Salah*. Once the servant completes his/her questioning for *Salah* with success, the rest of the interrogation becomes easier.

Qur'an is the greatest evidence for this. The Holy Qur'an informs us that *Salah* keeps believers away from evil and indecency. *Salah* is the most virtuous deed by the side of Allah. Once, a man asked the Prophet about the most virtuous deed. The Prophet stated that the most virtuous deed is the Prescribed Prayer. The man asked again and again. For the first three times, the noble Prophet repeated, "The Prayer"[15]

Muslims must remember that *Salah* is not a custom; it is a unique act of worship prescribed by Allah himself. *Salah* cannot be altered and there are no alternatives to it. Although, some compulsory acts of worship can sometimes be abandoned with valid excuse, *Salah* cannot be abandoned under any circumstances. Even the traveler and the ill are required to perform the five Daily Prayers. During the time of the noble Prophet, they performed *Salah* even during battles. The significance of *Salah* is described quite explicitly in the following *hadith*: "The place of *Salah* in religion is like the place of the head in the human body.[16]

The five Daily Prayers also play a great role in sin prevention. It is quite difficult for a believer who has performed his/her Noon Prayer to commit an evil deed, knowing that he/she will stand before his/her Lord again during the Afternoon Prayer which is only a few hours away. The main reason for this is:

Salah is a Divine light that enters the heart each time the servant of Allah performs it. Consequently, darkness

---

[15] Ahmad ibn Hanbal, *Musnad*, XIII.352.

[16] Al-Tabarani, *Al-Mu'jam al-Kabir*, IX.94.

cannot survive in the same environment where there is light. Hence, hearts illuminated by *Salah* will abstain from evil thoughts. This notion is strengthened by a verse from the Holy Qur'an:

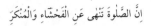

Verily, Salah prevents shameless and evil deeds.[17]

The most important thing that the All-Merciful Allah requests from us is gratitude. There are many ways of thanking our Lord for all the bounties He has bestowed upon us; however, *Salah* is the most complete and the most profound way of displaying one's appreciation. Those who wish to obtain happiness and contentment in both worlds should steadfastly observe the five Daily Prayers.

The Prescribed Prayers are offered five times a day and they are as follows:

- The Morning Prayer (Fajr)
- The Noon Prayer (Zuhr)
- The Afternoon Prayer (Asr)
- The Evening Prayer (Maghrib)
- The Night Prayer (Isha)

All of the obligatory Prayers have designated times that should be followed with total care...

In addition to the Daily Prayers there is the Friday Prayer which is also obligatory for all male Muslims who are sane, free, over the age of adolescence and healthy

---

[17] Qur'an: 29:45.

enough to perform it. As explained above, the Prescribed Prayers have designated times and it is imperative for Muslims to perform their Prayers on time.

In his master piece, *The Words*, Bediüzzaman Said Nursi explains the significance of the designated times of the five Prescribed Daily Prayers:

* * *

In the Name of Allah, the All-Merciful, the All-Compassionate.

فَسُبْحَانَ اللهِ حِينَ تُمْسُونَ وَحِينَ تُصْبِحُونَ ۞ وَلَهُ الْحَمْدُ فِى السَّمٰوَاتِ وَالْاَرْضِ وَعَشِيًّا وَحِينَ تُظْهِرُونَ

So glorify Allah when you reach evening and when you rise in the morning; for all praise is His in the heavens and on earth, and towards the end of the day and when you have reached noon.[18]

Brothers (sisters)! You ask me concerning the wisdom in the specified times of the five Daily Prayers. I shall point out only one of the many instances of wisdom in the times.

Indeed, like each of the times of Prayer marks the start of an important revolution, so also is each a mirror to Divine disposal of power and to the universal Divine bounties within that disposal. Thus, more glorification and extolling of the All-Powerful One of Glory have been ordered at those times, and more praise and thanks for all the innumerable bounties accumulated between each of the times, which is the meaning of the Prescribed Prayers. In order to understand a little this subtle and profound

---

[18] Qur'an.30:17–18.

meaning, you should listen together with my own soul to the following 'Five Points'.

First Point

The meaning of the Prayers is the offering of glorification, praise, and thanks to Almighty Allah. That is to say, uttering Glory be to Allah by word and action before Allah's glory and sublimity, it is to. Hallow and worship Him. And declaring Allah is Most Great through word and act before His sheer perfection, it is to exalt and magnify Him. And saying all praise be to Allah with the heart, tongue, and body, it is to offer thanks before His utter beauty. That is to say, glorification, exaltation, and praise are like the seeds of the Prayers. That is why these three things are present in every part of the Prayers, in all the actions and words. And it is also why these blessed words are each repeated thirty-three times after the Prayers, in order to strengthen and reiterate the Prayers' meaning. The meaning of the Prayers is confirmed through these concise summaries.

Second Point

The meaning of worship is this, that the servant sees his own faults, impotence. And poverty, and in the Divine Court prostrates in love and wonderment before Divine perfection, Divine mercy, and the power of the Eternally Besought One. That is to say, just as the sovereignty of Lordship demands worship and obedience, so also does the holiness of Lordship require that the servant sees his faults through seeking forgiveness, and through his glori-fications and declaring Glory be to Allah proclaims that his Sustainer is pure and free of all defects, and exalted above and far from the false ideas of the people of mis-guidance, and hallowed and exempt from all the faults in the universe.

And the perfect power of Lordship requires that through understanding his own weakness and the impo-tence of other creatures, the servant proclaims Allah is Most Great in admiration and wonder before the majesty of the works of the Eternally Besought One's power, and bowing in deep humility seeks refuge in Him and places his trust in Him.

And the infinite treasury of Lordship's mercy requires that the servant makes known his own need and the needs and poverty of all creatures through the tongue of ques-tioning and supplication, and proclaims his Sustainer's bounties and gifts through thanks and laudation and utter-ing All praise be to Allah. That is to say, the words and actions of the Prayers comprise these meanings, and have been laid down from the side of Divinity.

Third Point

Just as man is an example in miniature of the greater world and *Surah al-Fatiha* a shining sample of the Qur'an of Mighty Stature, so too are the Prescribed Prayers a com-prehensive and luminous index of all varieties of worship, and a sacred map pointing to all the shades of worship of all the classes of creatures.

Fourth Point

Just as the second-hand, minute-hand, hour-hand, and day-hand of a clock which tells the weeks look to one another, are examples of one another, and follow one another, so too the revolutions of day and night, which are like the seconds of this world—a vast clock of Almighty Allah—and the years which tell its minutes, and the stages of man's life-span which tell the hours, and the epochs of the world's life-span which tell the days look to one another, are examples of one another, are like one another, and recall one another. For example:

The time of Fajr, the early morning: This time until sunrise resembles and calls to mind the early spring, the moment of conception in the mother's womb, and the first of the six days of the creation of the heavens and earth; it recalls the Divine acts present in them.

The time of Zuhr, just past midday: This resembles and points to midsummer, and the prime of youth, and the period of man's creation in the lifetime of the world, and calls to mind the manifestations of mercy and the abundant bounties in them.

The time of Asr, afternoon: This is like autumn, and old age, and the time of the Final Prophet (pbuh), known as the Era of Bliss, and recalls the Divine acts and favors of the All-Merciful One in them.

The time of Maghrib, sunset: Through recalling the departure of many creatures at the end of autumn, and man's death, and the destruction of the world at the commencement of the Resurrection, this time puts in mind the manifestations of Divine Glory and Sublimity, and rouses man from his slumbers of heedlessness.

The time of 'Isha, nightfall: As for this time, by calling to mind the world of darkness veiling all the objects of the daytime world with a black shroud, and winter hiding the face of the dead earth with its white cerement, and even the remaining works of departed men dying and passing beneath the veil of oblivion, and this world, the arena of examination, being shut up and closed down for ever, it proclaims the awesome and mighty disposals of the All-Glorious and Compelling Subduer.

As for *the nighttime*, through putting in mind both the winter, and the grave, and the Intermediate Realm, it reminds man how needy is the human spirit for the Most Merciful One's Mercy. And the *Tahajjud* Prayer informs him what a necessary light it is for the night of the grave and darkness of the Intermediate Realm; it warns him of this, and through recalling the infinite bounties of the True Bestower, proclaims how deserving He is of praise and thanks.

And *the second morning* calls to mind the Morning of the Resurrection. For sure, however reasonable and necessary and certain the morning of this night is, the Morning of the Resurrection and the spring following the Intermediate Realm are that certain.

That is, just as each of these five times marks the start of an important revolution and recalls other great revolutions, so too through the awesome daily disposals of the Eternally Besought One's power, each calls to mind the miracles of Divine power and gifts of Divine mercy of both every year, and every age, and every epoch. That is to say, the Prescribed Prayers, which are an innate duty and the basis of worship and an incontestable debt, are most appropriate and fitting for these times.

Fifth Point

By nature man is extremely weak, yet everything touches him, and saddens and grieves him. Also he is utterly lacking in power, yet the calamities and enemies that afflict him are extremely numerous. Also he is extremely wanting, yet his needs are indeed many. Also he is lazy and incapable, yet life's responsibilities are most burdensome. Also his humanity has connected him to the rest of the universe, yet the decline and disappearance of the things he loves and with which he is familiar continually pains him. Also his reason shows him exalted aims and lasting fruits, yet his hand is short, his life brief, his power slight, and his patience little.

Thus, it can be clearly understood how essential it is for a spirit in this state at the time of Fajr in the early morning to have recourse to and present a petition to the Court of an All-Powerful One of Glory, an All-Compassionate All-Beauteous One through Prayer and supplication, to seek success and help from Him, and what a necessary point of support it is so that he can face the things that will happen to him in the coming day and bear the duties that will be loaded on him.

And the time of *Zuhr* just past midday Is the time of the day's zenith and the start of its decline ? the time when daily labors approach their achievement, the time of a short rest from the pressures of work, when the spirit needs a pause from the heedlessness and insensibility caused by toil, and a time Divine bounties are manifest. Anyone may understand then how fine and agreeable, how necessary and appropriate it is to perform the Midday Prayer for the human spirit, which means to be released from the pressure, shake off the heedlessness, and leave behind those meaningless, transient things, and clasping one hands at the Court of the True Bestower of Bounties, the Eternally Self-Subsistent One, to offer praise and thanks for all His gifts, and seek help from Him, and through bowing to display one's impotence before His Glory and Tremendousness, and to prostrate and proclaim one's wonder, love, and humility. He who does not understand this is not a true human being...

As for the time of *Asr* in the afternoon, it calls to mind the melancholy season of autumn and the mournful state of old age and the somber period at the end of time. Also it is when the matters of the day reach their conclusion, and the time the Divine bounties which have been received that day like health, well-being, and beneficial duties have accumulated to form a great total, and the time that proclaims through the mighty sun hinting by starting to sink that man is a guest-official and that everything is transient and inconstant. Now, the human spirit desires eternity and was created for it; it worships benevolence, and is pained by separation. Thus, anyone who is truly a human being may understand what an exalted duty, what an appropriate service, whit a fitting way to repay a debt of human nature, indeed, what an agreeable pleasure it is to perform the Afternoon Prayer, for by offering supplications at the Eternal Court of the Everlasting Pre-Eternal One, the Eternally Self-Subsistent One, it has the meaning of taking refuge in the grace of unending, infinite Mercy, and by offering thanks and praise in the face of innumerable bounties, of humbly bowing before the Mightiness of His Lordship, and by prostrating in utter humility before the Everlastingness of His Divinity, of finding true consolation and ease of spirit, and being girded ready for worship in the presence of His Grandeur.

And the time of *Maghrib* at sunset recalls the disappearance amid sad farewells of the delicate and lovely creatures of the worlds of summer and autumn at the start of winter. And it calls to mind the time when through his death, man will leave all those he loves in sorrowful departure and enter the grave. And it brings to mind when at the death of this world amid the upheavals of its death-agonies, all its inhabitants will migrate to other worlds and the lamp of this place of examination will be extinguished. And it is a time which gives stern warning to those who worship transient, ephemeral beloveds.

Thus, at such a time, for the *Maghrib* Prayer, man's spirit, which by its nature is a mirror desirous for an Eternal Beauty, turns its face towards the throne of mightiness of the Eternal Undying One, the Enduring Everlasting

One, Who performs these mighty works and turns and transforms these huge worlds, and declaring Cod is Most Create over these transient beings, withdraws from them. Man clasps his hands in service of his Lord and rises in the presence of the Enduring Eternal One, and through saying: All praise be to Allah, he praises and extols His faultless perfection, His peerless beauty, His infinite mercy. And through declaring: اِيَّاكَ نَعْبُدُ وَاِيَّاكَ نَسْتَعِينُ *"You alone do we worship and from You alone we seek help,"*[19] he proclaims his worship for and seeks help from His unassisted Lordship, His unpartnered Divinity, His unshared sovereignty. Then he bows, and through declaring together with the entire universe his weakness and impotence, his poverty and baseness before the infinite majesty, the limitless power, and utter mightiness of the Enduring Eternal One, he says: All glory to My Mighty Sustainer, and glorifies his Sublime Sustainer. And prostrating before the undying Beauty of His Essence, His unchanging sacred Attributes, His constant everlasting perfection, through abandoning all things other than Him, man proclaims his love and worship in wonder and self-abasement, he finds an All-Compassionate Eternal One, and through saying, All glory to my Exalted Sustainer, he declares his Most High Sustainer to be free of decline and exalted above any fault.

Then, he testifies to Allah's Unity and the Prophethood of Muhammad. He sits, and on his own account offers as a gift to the Undying All-Beauteous One, the Enduring All-

---

[19] Qur'an: 1:5.

Glorious One the blessed salutations and benedictions of all creatures. And through greeting the Most Noble Prophet, he renews his allegiance to him and proclaims his obedience to his commands. In order to renew and illuminate his faith, he observes the wise order in this palace of the universe and testifies to the Unity of the All-Glorious Maker. And he testifies to the Prophethood of Muhammad the Arabian, peace and blessings be upon him, who is the herald of the sovereignty of Allah's Lordship, the proclaimer of those things pleasing to Him, and the interpreter of the signs and verses of the Book of the Universe. To perform the Maghrib Prayer is this. Thus, how can someone be considered to be a human being who does not understand what a fine and pure duty is the Prayer at sunset, what an exalted and pleasurable act of service, what an agreeable and pleasing act of worship, what a serious matter, and what an unending conversation and permanent happiness it is in this transient guest-house?

And at the time of 'Isha at nightfall, the last traces of the day remaining on the horizon disappear, and the world of night encloses the universe. As the All-Powerful and Glorious One, The Changer of Night and Day, turns the white page of day into the black one of night through the mighty disposals of His Lordship, it recalls the Divine activities of that All-Wise One of Perfection, The Subduer of the Sun and the Moon, turning the green adorned page of summer into the frigid white page of winter. And with the remaining works of the departed being erased from this world with the passing of time, it recalls the Divine acts of The

Creator and Life and Death in their passage to another, quite different world. It is a time that calls to mind the disposals of The Creator of the Heavens and the Earth's Awesomeness and the manifestations of His Beauty in the utter destruction of this narrow, fleeting, and lowly world, the terrible death-agonies of its decease, and in the unfolding of the broad, eternal, and majestic World of the Hereafter. And the universe's Owner, its True Disposer, its True Beloved and Object of Worship can only be the One Who with ease turns night into day, winter into spring, and this world into the Hereafter like the pages of a book; Who writes and erases them, and changes them.

Thus, at nightfall, man's spirit, which is infinitely impotent and weak, and infinitely poor and needy, and plunged into the infinite darkness of the future, and tossed around amid innumerable events, performs the 'Isha Prayer, which has this meaning: Like Abraham man says: لَآ اُحِبُّ الْاٰفِلِينَ *"I do not love those that set,"*[20] and through the Prayers seeks refuge at the Court of an Undying Object of Worship, an Eternal Beloved One, and in this transient world and fleeting life and dark world and black future he supplicates an Enduring, Everlasting One, and for a moment of unending conversation, a few seconds of immortal life, he asks to receive the favours of the All-Merciful and Compassionate One's Mercy and the light of His guidance, which will strew light on his world and illuminate his future and bind up the

---

[20] Qur'an: 6:76.

wounds resulting from the departure and decline of all creatures and friends.

And temporarily man forgets the hidden world, which has forgotten him, and pours out his woes at the Court of Mercy with his weeping, and whatever happens, before sleeping—which resembles death—he performs his last duty of worship. And in order to close favorably the daily record of his actions, he rises to pray; that is to say, he rises to enter the presence of an Eternal Beloved and Worshipped One in place of all the mortal ones he loves, of an All-Powerful and Generous One in place of all the impotent creatures from which he begs, of an All-Compassionate Protector so as to be saved from the evil of the harmful beings before which he trembles.

And he starts with the Fatiha, that is, instead of praising and being obliged to defective, wanting creatures, for which they are not suited, he extols and offers praise to The Sustainer of All the Worlds, Who is Absolutely Perfect and Utterly Self-Sufficient and Most Compassionate and All Generous. Then he progresses to the address: You alone do we worship. That is, despite his smallness, insignificance, and aloneness, through man's connection with The Owner of the Day of Judgment, Who is the Sovereign of Pre-Eternity and Post-Eternity, he attains to a rank whereat he is an indulged guest in the universe and an important official. Through declaring: You alone do we worship and from You alone do we seek help, he presents to Him in the name of all creatures the worship and calls for assistance of the mighty congregation and huge community of the universe.

Then through saying: Guide us to the Straight Path, he asks to be guided to the Straight Path, which leads to eternal happiness and is the luminous way.

And now, he thinks of the mightiness of the All-Glorious One, of Whom, like the sleeping plants and animals, the hidden suns and sober stars are each as though a soldier subjugated to His command, and a lamp and servant in this guest-house of the world, and uttering: Allah is Most Great, he bows down. Then he thinks of the great prostration of all creatures. That is, when, at the command of *Be! and it is*,[21] all the varieties of creatures each year and each century—and even the Earth, and the universe—each like a well ordered army or an obedient soldier, is discharged from its duty, that is, when each is sent to the World of the Unseen, through the prostration of its decease and death with complete orderliness, it declares: Allah is Most Create, and bows down in prostration. And like they are raised to life, some in part and some the same, in the spring at an awakening and life-giving trumpet blast from the Command of Be! and it is, and they rise up and are girded ready to serve their Lord, insignificant man too, following them, declares: Allah is Most Great! in the presence of the All-Merciful One of Perfection, the All-Compassionate One of Beauty in wonder struck love and eternity tinged humility and dignified self-effacement, and bows down in prostration; that is to say, he makes a sort of Ascension And for sure you will have understood now

---

21 Qur'an: 2:117, and others.

how agreeable and fine and pleasant and elevated, how high and pleasurable, how reasonable and appropriate a duty, service, and act of worship, and what a serious matter it is to perform the 'Isha Prayer.

Thus, since each of these five times is an indication to a mighty revolution, a sign to the tremendous Dominicial activity, and a token of the universal Divine bounties, the Prescribed Prayers, which are a debt and an obligation, being specified at them is perfect wisdom...

سُبْحَانَكَ لَا عِلْمَ لَنَا اِلَّا مَا عَلَّمْتَنَا اِنَّكَ اَنْتَ الْعَلِيمُ الْحَكِيمُ

> *Glory be unto You! We have no knowledge save that which You have taught us; indeed You are All-Knowing, All-Wise.*[22]

O Allah! Grant blessings and peace to the one whom You sent as a teacher to Your servants to instruct them in knowledge of You and worship of You, and to make known the treasures of Your Names, and to translate the signs of the Book of the [Universe and as a mirror to its worship of the beauty of Your Lordship, and to all his Family and Companions, and have Mercy on us and on all believing men and women. Amen. Through Your Mercy, O Most Merciful of the Merciful![23]

---

[22] Qur'an: 2:32.
[23] Said Nursi: Risale-i Nur Collection, *The Words*, The Ninth Word.

THE RAMADAN FAST

شَهْرُ رَمَضَانَ الَّذِى اُنْزِلَ فِيهِ الْقُرْاٰنُ هُدًى لِلنَّاسِ وَبَيِّنَاتٍ مِنَ الْهُدٰى وَالْفُرْقَانِ فَمَنْ شَهِدَ مِنْكُمُ الشَّهْرَ فَلْيَصُمْهُ وَمَنْ كَانَ مَرِيضاً اَوْ عَلٰى سَفَرٍ فَعِدَّةٌ مِنْ اَيَّامٍ اُخَرَ

The month of Ramadan in which was revealed the Qur'an, a guidance for mankind and clear proofs for the guidance and the criterion (between right and wrong). So whoever of you sights (the crescent on the first night of) the month (of Ramadan), he must fast that month, and whoever is ill or on a journey, the same number (of days which one did not fast must be made up) from other days.[24]

Ramadan is the holiest month in the Muslim calendar. It is the ninth month of the Islamic calendar which follows the lunar cycle. Months in the Islamic calendar begin when the first crescent of a new moon is sighted. Therefore, Ramadan, the month of fasting begins immediately after the new moon is sighted. Ramadan is a month in which all Muslims, healthy, sane and over the age of adolescence is obligated to observe the fast each day of the month of Ramadan from sunrise to sunset. Fasting begins just before dawn with a meal called *Sahur*. Following the meal, the believer makes the inten-

---

[24] Qur'an: 2:185.

tion to fast and until sunset he/she abstains from all forms of food, drink and sexual activities. Fasting is the third pillar of Islam and it is a worship rewarded by Allah himself.

Fasting has many benefits. These benefits can be summarized as physical, spiritual and social benefits. Although, extensive research proves that fasting is the most extraordinary way of cleansing the body off toxins and harmful substances, one must remember that fasting is not a form of diet or self-starvation. It is a prescribed worship that also encompasses self-discipline. However, in order to illustrate the benefits of fasting, we also need to explain its physical benefits. Therefore, we shall first look into its dietary benefits.

1. Physical Benefits of Fasting

In his book, 'Fruits of Worship' Abdullah Aymaz explains:

> Converting food and other substances into required energy and into living tissue is not a simple process. As soon as a morsel of food enters the mouth, all digestion sensors are activated. With the support of the central nervous system and the nerves that function to aid digestion of food, and related muscles and discharge glands go into action.
>
> Once the necessary digestion process is completed in the mouth, the mashed up food is then sent to the stomach via a determined nerve reflex. The second phase of digestion is completed by the stomach that goes into action with reflex muscle movements and discharge of fluids. Following the third phase of digestion completed by the small intestines, the food is ready to be absorbed. The liver also goes into

action to perform more than 450 of its various functions. The heart then takes on a duty several times more than its usual functioning rate. All of the small and large organs of the body, including its cells take part in this strenuous process.

It is because of this exhausting process of digestion that the heart and other organs of the body become fatigued and the necessary amount of blood is not sent to the central nerve cells of the brain. It is obvious that overeating exerts an incredible amount of pressure on the body and its organs.

This is the main reason as to why people who eat too much hence fail to follow a good diet do not live long. Every organ possesses a capacity to last for a certain time. When overworked, they lose their functionality and age rapidly.

For this reason, people who eat less, live long. It is as if their youth continues throughout their lives. This is why fasting is extremely beneficial to our health. Moreover, fasting strengthens the body's immune system and protects it from illnesses.

Modern medicine and preventative health uses fasting as a means of protection against certain illnesses. Some stubborn illnesses are fought with fasting. Indeed, the great benefits of fasting and healthy diet are quite evident. These days, we witness that all doctors support their prescriptions with a diet list which describes what the patient should eat or should not eat. Modern medicine has realized the connection between illnesses and unhealthy diet. Muslims are well aware of the following advice; "Stomach is the home of illnesses and a proper diet is the best medicine". The Islamic principle: "observes the fast and remain strong" is interpreted by modern science as, "Fast and remain healthy".

This is exactly what we mean when we say, "Fasting prolongs life". Certainly, the duration of life is in the hands of Allah. Even the healthiest person could die within a matter of hours. Modern science cannot alter the will of Allah. However, Divine will is aware of all causes and reasons hence as it decides; it also takes these issues into account. Fasting is an effective method in the treatment of chronic intestine disorders. It is also used in the treatment of constipation. Some other medical benefits of fasting are: The treatment of some skin disorders and the resting of stomach and intestines. Foods containing albumin produce acids and vegetables produce various bases. In turn, these substances synthesize to produce various salts. There are many different salts in our cells and tissues. If there is insufficient base in our diet, acids will not be converted to salts and this is the first sign of poisoning. Although the body has certain reserves to balance this out, if the condition reoccurs, it will lead to health problems. Fifty percent of illnesses are caused by stomach disorders. Even though the balance of acids, bases and salts is quite imperative, we do not eat to control this balance. On the contrary, our eating habits depend on our taste or budget. The body needs an annual resting period, at least for a month, in order to protect itself from this unbalanced diet. The prescribed Islamic fasting breaks up the harmful fats that surround our inner organs. Fasting is similar to the process of pruning trees hence human metabolism goes through a revitalization process. Through fasting, body's resistance increases towards certain illnesses such as diabetes, kidney and liver disorders, cardiac and artery problems, as long as there is no overeating involved during *Sahur* and *Iftar*.[25]

It is apparent that fasting offers many benefits to human body but as explained earlier, it is not a form of diet or self-starvation. During the Ramadan fast, Muslims are not only asked to refrain from eating and drinking but also asked to abstain from temptations of the flesh and all types of evil deeds. Although, Muslims are encouraged to refrain from all types of wrongdoings throughout their lives, during Ramadan the sensitivity levels towards sins increase drastically. The Ramadan fast can be considered as a form of self-discipline encompassing both the body and soul. Therefore, the spiritual benefits of fasting are more significant than its physical benefits.

2. Spiritual Benefits of Fasting

Human beings are composed of two essential components, the body and the soul. The body is the physical-animalistic side of human nature. It is mainly motored by a property called the *'Nafs'* (carnal self). *Nafs* recognizes no barriers and always assumes that it has complete freedom to do as it wishes. In a sense, it visualizes a false Lordship in itself. It does not think about the origin of the countless bounties it receives in life. The more the blessings, the more it wants without realizing that it is being tested by the Almighty.

A humorous analogy suggests that if you give the deed of the entire planet earth to a human *nafs*, before long it will develop a desire for the other planets in the solar system.

---

[25] Abdullah Aymaz, *İbadetin Getirdikleri*, Işık Yayınları, 1997.

The human carnal desire becomes more and more demanding as it accumulates more wealth and power. It does not like authority, rules or regulations. It takes but does not thank. In particular, the carnal desire of those who have no appreciation for the 'Divine Hand' that bestows all sustenance, transforms into a pharaoh-like entity which believes it has the authority to take whatever it wishes.

As the Holy Qur'an describes:

$$\text{يَأْكُلُونَ كَمَا تَأْكُلُ الْأَنْعَامُ}$$

They consume (Allah's bounties) like animals.[26]

During the holy month of Ramadan however, the human carnal desire realizes that it is not the sovereign but a mere servant. Without the permission of the true King, it cannot reach for a morsel of bread or a drop of water. It realizes its freedom is limited. It acknowledges its vulnerability, weakness and impotence. It contemplates about where the food comes from and begins to feel grateful. Eventually, this gratitude leads to submission.

During Ramadan, the entire Muslim world transforms into a place of worship where all servants of Allah wait for the commandment to eat. The carnal desire concedes that it too is a weak, impotent servant of Allah who can only survive through the bounties sent by the All-Merciful. Then it enters into a period of self-discipline, obedience and submission. It is through this period of self-discipline,

---

[26] Qur'an: 47:12.

the soul takes control of the carnal desire. At the completion of Ramadan, a new human being emerges, an individual that has the ability to control his/her eating habits, behavior, anger, rage and sexual desires. Ramadan can be considered as a miraculous one-month program for self-discipline, personal development and spiritual enhancement. No other method on earth could provide such amazing results within such short period of time. From a psychological point of view, Ramadan fast is a process of anger management, rehabilitation, self improvement and a program that teaches individuals to control their eating habits. Statistics show amazing results in relation to issues above particularly in the Muslim world. Crime rates during Ramadan drop significantly in all Muslim countries. Many people kick bad habits such as alcohol consumption and smoking during Ramadan. Family members, relatives, neighbors and local communities interact with each other more often during Ramadan hence establish stronger bonds and mutual support.

The month of Ramadan is also a spiritual trading ground where believers get the opportunity to engage in highly profitable spiritual business dealings that concern the life after death. Since all Divine rewards increase drastically during Ramadan, it encourages the soul to perform more good deeds and worship. This in turn enables one to accumulate more rewards for the life after. According to a verse, a single night in Ramadan can earn eighty years of worship rewards. The evidence is in the Qur'an which informs us the night of *Qadr*[27] is equal to one thousand months of blessings. Consequently, there are many benefits in fasting during Ramadan.

The most faultless and beneficial way of fasting, however, is the one in which the worshipper fasts with his/her tongue, eyes, ears, heart, imagination and emotions just as he/she does with his/her stomach. This means refraining from all forms of religious prohibitions and ineffectual acts by fasting with all senses and emotions. Those who achieve this will receive the highest benefits from the spiritual blessings of Ramadan.

One of the most important spiritual benefits of Ramadan is that it is a month of cultivation for eternal rewards. This is explained magnificently, in the twenty-ninth letter of the *Letters (Risale Nur Collection)* authored by the great Islamic scholar Bediüzzaman Said Nursi:

> The Twenty-Ninth Letter, seventh point
>
> One of the many instances of wisdom in the fast of Ramadan with respect to mankind's gain and profit, who comes to this world in order to cultivate and trade for the hereafter, is as follows:
>
> The reward for actions in the month of Ramadan is a thousand fold. According to Hadith, each word of the All-Wise Qur'an has ten merits; each is counted as ten merits and will yield ten fruits in Paradise. While during Ramadan, each word bears not ten fruits but a thousand, and verses like *Ayat al-Kursi* thousands for each word, and on Fridays in Ramadan it is even

---

[27] Qur'an: 97:3.

more. And on the Night of Power, each word is counted as thirty thousand merits.

Indeed, the All-Wise Qur'an, each of whose words yield thirty thousand eternal fruits, is like a luminous Tree of Tuba that gains for believers in Ramadan millions of those eternal fruits. So, come and look at this sacred, eternal profitable trade, then consider it and understand the infinite loss of those who do not appreciate the value of those words.

To put it simply, the month of Ramadan is an extremely profitable display and market for the trade of the hereafter. It is an extremely fertile piece of land for the crops of the hereafter. For the growth and flourishing of actions it is like April showers in the spring. It is like a brilliant holy festival for the parade of mankind's worship in the face of the sovereignty of Divine dominicality. Since it is thus, mankind has been charged with fasting in order not to heedlessly indulge the animal needs of the instinctual soul like eating and drinking, nor to indulge the appetites lustfully and in trivialities. For, by temporarily rising above animality and quitting the calls of this world, man approaches the angelic state and enters upon the trade of the hereafter. And by fasting, he approaches the state of the hereafter and that of a spirit appearing in bodily form. It is as if man then becomes a sort of mirror reflecting the Eternally Besought One. Indeed, the month of Ramadan comprises and gains a permanent and eternal life in this fleeting world and brief transient life.

Certainly, a single Ramadan can produce fruits equal to that of a lifetime of eighty years. The fact that, according to the Qur'an, the Night of Power is more auspicious than a thousand months is a decisive proof of this.

For example, a monarch may declare certain days to be festivals during his reign, or perhaps once a year. Either on his accession to the throne or on some other days which reflect a glittering manifestation of his sovereignty. On those days, he favours his subjects, not within the general sphere of the law, but with his special bounties and favours, with his presence without veil and his wondrous activities. And he favours with his especial regard and attention those of his nation who are completely loyal and worthy.

In the same way, the All-Glorious Monarch of eighteen thousand worlds, Who is the Sovereign of Pre-Eternity and Post-Eternity, revealed in Ramadan the illustrious decree of the All-Wise Qur'an, which looks to the eighteen thousand worlds. It is a requirement of wisdom, then, that Ramadan should be like special Divine festival, a dominical display, and a spiritual gathering. Since Ramadan is such festival, Allah has commanded man to fast, in order to disengage him to a degree from base and animal activities.

The most excellent fasting is to make the human senses and organs, like the eyes, ears, heart, and thoughts, fast together with the stomach. That is, to withdraw them from all unlawful things and from trivia, and to urge each of them to their particular worship.

For example, to ban the tongue from lying, backbiting, and obscene language and to make it fast. And to busy it with activities like reciting the Qur'an, praying, glorifying Allah's Names, asking for Allah's blessings on Prophet Muhammad, peace and blessings be upon him, and seeking forgiveness for sins. And for example, to prevent the eyes looking at members of the opposite sex outside the stipulated degrees of kinship, and the ears from hearing harmful things, and to use the eyes to take lessons and the ears to listen to the truth and to the Qur'an, is to make other organs fast too. As a matter of fact, since the stomach is the largest factory, if it has an enforced holiday from work through fasting, the other small workshops will be made to follow it easily.[28]

3. Social Benefits of Fasting

Ramadan is also a month of empathy. It is a month in which the more fortunate and the privileged experience the feeling of hunger and starvation. This is a feeling they could never realize or experience without fasting. The agony of hunger and thirst develops empathy and compassion in their hearts and soul. Realizing how the poor live and survive, they feel a compelling need to help. In regards to the psychological development of this empathy, Abdullah Aymaz states:

> Without fasting, some selfish wealthy individuals would not comprehend the extreme difficulties endured by the needy and how much compassion they need. People who have full stomachs will not show empathy towards those who are starving, unless they experience the feeling by refraining from food, themselves. Therefore, fasting is the most suitable thing for this.

> Tackling the issue from this perspective, empathy towards fellow human beings is the essence of a genuine gratitude. No matter how poor you are, there will always be someone poorer. Therefore, you are responsible of displaying compassion to that person. Unless individuals become obligated to experience hunger, they will not fulfill the responsibility of

---

[28] Said Nursi, The *Letters: The Twenty-Ninth Letter*.

helping others. Even if they did, it will not be complete, because they do not feel their suffering.[29]

It is this empathy and religious obligation that encourages the wealthy to help the less-fortunate, makes Ramadan a month of social support and harmony. Additionally, the tradition of *Iftar* dinners eaten with guests during Ramadan evenings brings people from all walks of life around the same table to break bread together while they interact with each other. In turn, this develops social inclusiveness and harmony. It breaks down the barriers of prejudice, bigotry and discrimination.

Iftar dinners also play a significant role in the promotion of intercultural and interfaith dialogue. Since, it is an important tradition of Ramadan to break the fast with relatives, friends, neighbours and people in the community, Muslims are encouraged to invite people of other faiths and cultures to their dining tables for the Iftar dinners. This provides the opportunity for non-Muslims to interact with Muslims and learn about their culture and practices. Iftar dinners promote social inclusiveness hence encourage the establishment of solid, lasting friendships.

In conclusion, fasting, the third pillar of Islam is observed in Ramadan, a month in which physical, spiritual and social blessings and benefits are bestowed in abundance. Those who reach it should make the most of it because it is unknown whether one would make it to the following Ramadan...

---

[29] Abdullah Aymaz, *İbadetin Getirdikleri*, Işık Yayınları, 1997.

Zakah
(The Prescribed Purifying Alms)

وَاَقِيمُوا الصَّلٰوةَ وَاٰتُوا الزَّكٰوةَ

And be steadfast in Prayer; practice regular charity.[30]

Z akah is the fourth pillar of Islam and in the Qur'an all the verses regarding alms-giving, mention *Zakah* straight after mentioning the obligatory Prayers. *Zakah* is the most perfect social welfare system that protects the giver from thriftiness and saves the poor and the needy from the humiliation of poverty and starvation. The Holy Qur'an explains this quite overtly:

اِنَّمَا الصَّدَقَاتُ لِلْفُقَرَّاءِ وَالْمَسَاكِينِ وَالْعَامِلِينَ عَلَيْهَا وَالْمُؤَلَّفَةِ قُلُوبُهُمْ وَفِى الرِّقَابِ وَالْغَارِمِينَ وَفِى سَبِيلِ اللهِ وَابْنِ السَّبِيلِ فَرِيضَةً مِنَ اللهِ وَاللهُ عَلِيمٌ حَكِيمٌ

Alms are for the poor and the needy, and those employed to administer the (funds); for those whose hearts have been (recently) reconciled (to Truth); for those in bondage and in debt; in the cause of Allah; and for the wayfarer:

(thus is it) ordained by Allah, and Allah is full of knowledge and wisdom.[31]

Zakah is an act of worship and it is an obligatory act for all Muslims who are considered as wealthy by Islamic criterion. People who are required to give *Zakah* can be summarized as:

- The individual should be a Muslim, adult, sane and free.
- He/she must possess a certain minimum amount of additional wealth defined as *Nisab*, fully owned by them additional to personal possessions such as a home, clothing, food, household furniture, utensils and vehicles...
- This minimum amount should have been in possession for a complete year.
- The wealth should be of a productive or profitable nature, from which the possessor can make profits such as merchandise for trading, business, gold, silver, livestock, etc.
- This minimum amount should be debt free.

The mandatory *Zakah* amount is calculated as one fortieth of the extra wealth which equals to 2.5%. All Muslims who fit the above criterion are obligated to give *Zakah*, the obligatory alms on annual bases.

---

[31] Qur'an: 9:60.

There Are Spiritual, Social and Economical Aspects of *Zakah*

On a spiritual and personal level, a Muslim fulfills his/her obligation to Allah by giving *Zakah*. Through this act of worship the believer concedes that he/she is not the true owner of wealth. A wealthy believer admits to the fact that all wealth belongs to Allah thus it was entrusted upon the holder for a fix period of time. Moreover, the poor and the needy have rights over this transitory wealth. *Zakah* cleanses one's soul and purifies his/her wealth. It encourages one to be generous and munificent hence it cleanses the soul from thriftiness and parsimony. Furthermore, it purifies the wealth from unfairly earned cash and funds that may have mixed into the assets.

Giving alms draws the mercy and blessings of Allah. The noble Messenger once said:

لاَ تُحْصِي فَيُحْصِيَ اللهُ عَلَيْكِ

Do not withhold your money (from charity, for if you did so) Allah would withhold His blessings from you.[32]

In addition to the many spiritual and physical benefits, *Zakah* also brings many social and economical benefits. It is a bridge that regulates social harmony and order. It establishes social support and protects the society from rebellion and uprising. Islam prescribes *Zakah* as an obligatory act of worship and forbids usury. *Zakah* breaches the

---

[32] Bukhari: volume 2, Book 24, Number 513.

gap between the wealthy and the poor hence establishes social order. Through *Zakah* the wealthy does not belittle the needy and the poor does not develop feelings of animosity and hatred towards the rich. Therefore, *Zakah* protects the very fabric of society by establishing a harmonious bridge between the wealthy and the poor.

Zakah also strengthens the economy and brings movement to the markets. Since, *Zakah* is given from additional assets; it encourages the wealthy to put their money into work instead of stocking or freezing it in financial institutions. Or else the capital owner would lose one-fortieth of his/her additional wealth each year. This encourages trade and business hence it supports the economy.

There is Divine wisdom in making *Zakah* an obligatory act and there are countless benefits in the institution of alms-giving. However, the most and foremost important thing for a believer is that *Zakah* is a commandment of Allah and it is the fourth pillar of Islam. Therefore, all Muslims who are required to give *Zakah* must do so...

HAJJ (The Holy Pilgrimage)

Hajj, the holy pilgrimage, is the fifth pillar of Islam. Islamic scholars have stated the conditions of *hajj* being obligatory, which, if they are met, make it obligatory for a person to perform *hajj*, and without them *hajj* is not obligatory. There are five such conditions: being Muslim, being sane, being an adult, being free and having the means and ability to perform it.

In *Fruits of Worship*, Abdullah Aymaz states:

> The worship of Hajj has two aspects: one relates to our individual side and the other to social life. The individual aspect of Hajj, in particular, is quite important. The reason for this is Hajj is a form of worship and servanthood that is performed at the highest spiritual level. Just as a soldier appears before the king, the vizier and the generals on the king's festive day and receives honors and compliments, similarly, the pilgrim—even if he is an average member of society—has journeyed through the ranks and like a saint, he has been elevated to the highest level to stand before the Lord of the worlds, the Almighty Allah. He is honored with a universal worship. Obviously, the various ranks of the universal Lordship that becomes unlocked with the key of Hajj and the exalted horizons that can only be observed through the binoculars of Hajj and the thousands of believers from different races and ranks gathered by the principles of

Hajj, chanting *"Labbayk... Allahumma Labbayk"*, can satisfy the thirst, curiosity and awe of the spiritual circle of servanthood which constantly expands as it observes the ranks and manifestations of omnipotence and listens to the chanting of "Allah is the greatest... Allah is the greatest, with the imagination and the heart... Through Hajj, the believer can declare and testify to the spiritual ranks that manifests in his heart or vision, visits his imagination or mind. After Hajj, such a profound meaning can only be found at various exalted and universal levels in the Eid Prayers, Prayer for rain, in the Prayers performed during solar and lunar eclipses and in the Prayers performed in congregation. This is the mystery behind the principles of Islam, even if they are in the nature of Sunnah.[33]

One of the most important aspects of worship in Islam is the collective worship factor. For example, offering the Prayers collectively with a group increases the spiritual rewards by twenty-seven times. *Hajj* is the occasion where the greatest gathering of believers occurs. It is a beautiful manifestation of collective servanthood. During *hajj*, the Almighty Allah unites the tongues and hearts of believers who come from all regions of the world. Believers of all races, color and nationalities respond to the call of the Almighty with their unified recitations that echo throughout the holy lands. Their collective Prayers rise to the heavens above and through angels, they reach the Exalted Throne of Allah.

How could the All-Merciful turn down a prayer made by such a large group of believers?

---

[33] Abdullah Aymaz, *İbadetin Getirdikleri*, Işık Yayınları, 1997.

وَقَالَ رَبُّكُمُ ادْعُونِى اَسْتَجِبْ لَكُمْ

And your Lord said: "Invoke Me, (and ask Me for any-thing) I will respond to your (invocation)."[34]

Indeed, Allah answers all prayers, however, prayers and supplications offered by a congregation has a much better chance of being accepted. *Hajj* is the place where the largest group of believers gathers.

Visiting these holy lands where the noble Messenger and his beloved Companions lived and began to spread the word of Allah will no doubt revitalize and revive the heart and soul of any believer who wishes it. Indeed, Hajj renews one's pledge to Allah and strengthens the *Iman* (faith). Standing shoulder to shoulder with brothers from Asia, Africa, America, Europe and other regions of the world and interacting with them also strengthens the bonds of brotherhood and unity. It also gives Muslims from all over the world an opportunity to discuss their problems and needs with their fellow believers. It is a place where conflicts of the Muslim world can be solved and resolved.

Hajj is a practical medium where the equality of believers are established and confirmed. People from all backgrounds, educated and non-educated, general and soldier, scholar and student, ruler and citizen gather in a holy land where they are all equal before Allah. They put all differences aside and join in a universal prayer for the salvation of humanity.

---

[34] Qur'an: 40:60.

Hajj is also a great academy where believers learn patience and tolerance. *Hajj* trains its students to refrain from evil temptations of the flesh and the carnal soul.

This holy pilgrimage teaches submission and obedience. It encourages Muslims to be benevolent and munificent towards their brothers, sisters and all creatures of Allah. It trains Muslims to be generous, to give without asking anything in return.

Hajj reminds us of the struggle that people of Allah experienced for centuries. The struggle of Prophet *Ibrahim, Ismail, Hagar*, the noble Messenger and his beloved Companions are relived during this holy journey. There are many spiritual glad tidings about *hajj*.

The noble Prophet once stated:

> *Perform the obligation of Hajj. As water cleans out all filth, hajj cleans out all sins.*[35]

In another *hadith* the noble Messenger of Allah said:

> *An accepted hajj wipes out all sins.*[36]

In conclusion, *hajj* is one of the most important principles of Islam hence abandoning this significant pillar of Islam without a valid reason would mean turning one's back to the call of Allah and His Messenger. Therefore, all Muslims who possess the means and ability to perform

hajj should do so at least once in their lifetime.

---

[35] Al-Tabarani, *Al-Mu'jam al-awsat*, XI.230 (http://www.alSunna.com).
[36] Ahmad ibn Hanbal, *Musnad*, XXXI.307.

THE MEANING OF WORSHIP IN ISLAM

WORSHIP

In the Qur'an, Allah informs us that He has created the Jinn and the human beings so that they may worship Him (see 51:56). This means that worshipping Allah is the main purpose of creation. Without doubt, all living beings worship Him in their own unique way. Living creatures that do not possess intelligence, worship Allah through their natural disposition. For example, collecting pollen from thousands of different flowers and producing honey is a ritual of worship performed by the honeybee. Perhaps, the honeybee is not aware of the worship it is performing; nevertheless, it relentlessly continues to fulfill its mission in an obedient manner and with total submission.

Just as the honeybee, all non-intelligent living beings perform worship through their natural disposition. Moreover, even the inanimate matter worship Allah through the duties bestowed upon them. From the minute particles of an atom to giant galaxies that embellish the heavens above, all matter obeys the laws and principles created and enforced by the All-Powerful Allah. Therefore, they all worship Him in their own unique way.

There is however, an important difference between worship performed by non-intelligent beings and worship required of human beings. Human beings were given the inimitable gift of freewill. Freewill enables human beings to make a choice in regards to the way they live. Although the Holy Qur'an clearly commands human beings to worship Allah in a prescribed manner, the decision to obey or disobey is left to the freewill of the individual. However, the consequences of refusal are also explicitly described in the Holy Qur'an.

One of the most important issues that we need to understand is Allah does not need our worship. On the contrary, it is us who need worship. Just as our bodies need nutrients to survive, our soul needs worship to carry on. Worship is the nourishment of the human soul. Without it, the human soul will be weakened and the animalistic side of a human being will eventually take the reins. Once control is given to the flesh, its desires and temptations will never end. Gradually, the body will lose its spiritual component and in an attempt to satisfy the physical side, it will begin to exert all energy towards the flesh. So worship strengthens and treats the soul and gives meaning to human life. In this case it would be quite illogical to ask, "why does Allah insist on our worship, does He need it", just as it would be irrational to ask a doctor, "why do you insist that I take this medicine regularly and at certain times?" It is obvious that it is not the doctor who needs the medicine, but the patient.

The act of worship performed through self-awareness is an important element that distinguishes human beings from the animals. Through worship, we display our intentional obedience to Allah. It is a form of submission and recognition of His Might. It is also a display of total gratitude for the countless gifts and bounties bestowed by the Almighty Allah. Through worship the believer also makes a strong statement, claiming, "I submit only to You, O Lord! This head will only bow and go to the prostration position before You!" With this statement the believer declares that he/she will not become a slave to worldly temptations such as wealth, power, fame and fortune.

Worship is the only reason behind the creation of human beings. It is a bridge between the physical and metaphysical realms. It is a pathway to eternity, absolute contentment and spiritual satisfaction. The tranquility and serenity attained through worship can never be obtained through any other means. Worship and prayer heals all forms of spiritual ailments hence those who perform them in their true essence will not be taken prisoner by the meaningless depressions and melancholies of this transient world of materialism.

The time of worship is the time of reunion. It is a period in which the worshipper establishes a direct connection with his Lord. During worship, there are no mediators or intermediaries between the worshipper and his/her Creator. Those who perform their worship in its purest form become mirrors to the exalted Names. For them, worship is a ritual of obedience, submission and love. It is a period during which the materialistic aspects of this realm have no value. Only then they understand the true meaning of humanity and only then they discover the purpose of existence. Indeed, through worship and prayer the believer realizes the profound meaning of *Ahsani Taqwim* (being created in the best pattern).

The impeccable example of this can be observed in the Prayers of the noble Messenger. His Companions inform us that as he stood up for the Prayer, they could hear a noise coming from his chest which sounded as if volcanoes were erupting in him. During a Prayer he was so inspirational that it seemed as if you could observe the reflection of Allah on him. Another example is the Prayer of Ali ibn Abi Talib, may Allah be pleased with him. It is recorded that each time Ali prepared for the Prayer, in anticipation of standing before his Lord, his face would turn pale and he would begin to shake like the leaves of a palm tree.

SUNNAH: THE PROPHETIC TRADITION

SUNNAH: THE PROPHETIC TRADITION

قُلْ إِنْ كُنْتُمْ تُحِبُّونَ اللهَ فَاتَّبِعُونِي يُحْبِبْكُمُ اللهُ وَيَغْفِرْ لَكُمْ ذُنُوبَكُمْ وَاللهُ غَفُورٌ رَحِيمٌ

*Say (O Muhammad): "If you do love Allah, Follow me:
Allah will love you and forgive you your sins: For Allah is
Oft-Forgiving, Most Merciful."*[37]

P rophet Muhammad, peace and blessings be upon
him, the eternal sun of both worlds, carries the title
Habib Allah which means the beloved of Allah.
According to one *Hadith Qudsi*,[38] the universe was created
because of him. No one fears, loves and praises Allah more
than he. He is the perfect human being, a model of faith,
compassion, obedience, submission, piety, trustworthiness
and righteousness. He is the ultimate guide who shows the
path to contentment in this world and eternal happiness in
the one after. All roads that lead to paradise pass through
him. Attaining the love, compassion and mercy of Allah is
proportional to embracing the actions and doctrines of the

---

[37] Qur'an: 3:31.
[38] A Hadith Qudsi is a statement where the Prophet reports a statement
and he refers it directly to Allah.

noble Messenger. If a believer wishes to be loved by Allah, he/she must obey the noble Prophet.

In order to achieve this, one must first learn about the luminous life and practices of the noble Prophet. Consequently, this can only be achieved through the knowledge of *Hadith* and *Sunnah*. So, what is the definition of *Hadith* and *Sunnah*?

Hadith: is the record of the sayings of the Prophet. The sayings, conduct and endorsements of the Prophet make up the *Sunnah* of the noble Messenger. The *hadith* has come to supplement the Holy Qur'an as a second source of the Islamic rules and principles. After the Holy Qur'an, *hadith* is the second source from which the teachings and doctrines of Islam are obtained.

The Prophet not only preached the principles and rulings of Islam, but personally practiced his teachings in all aspects and affairs of life. He brought the religion of Allah to his people, which he meticulously practiced himself. He was the greatest role model and a sublime guide that humanity had ever seen. *Hadiths* are the main source that we learn about his wonderful life.

The life of no other man has been investigated or examined in such fine detail in the history of humanity. We have information about almost everything he did throughout his Prophethood. Even such fine details as how he walked, spoke, ate, smiled and wept are recorded in the *hadiths*. It is through the *hadith,* we learn how a believer should believe and practice his/her religion. *Hadiths* also teach us his *Sun-*

nah and the noble Messenger himself said that whoever embraced his *Sunnah* would join him in paradise.

In order to practice his *Sunnah* one must have knowledge about his noble life and practices. This invaluable knowledge and wisdom can only be obtained through the *hadiths*. The thousands of authenticated *hadiths* reported by most reliable individuals are indisputable source of information in relation to the *Sunnah* of the Prophet. The noble Prophet was the most beloved servant of Allah and emulating him will bring believers closer to Allah. Therefore, observing his *Sunnah* is the best method of following the Prophet and it is the most excellent way of displaying one's love towards the noble Messenger of Allah. According to a *hadith,* observing his *Sunnah* in this day . and age *(the End Times)* means being the recipients of a reward of one hundred martyrs. So, what is the exact definition of the word *Sunnah?*

Sunnah: Literally, it means a 'path', 'smooth path' or a 'clear path'. In relation to the *Sunnah* of Prophet Muhammad, it refers to the way of life which the noble Messenger of Allah lived and instructed believers to follow. As the above verse clearly indicates, following the noble Prophet leads to the love of Allah and cleansing from sins. Observing his *Sunnah* is imperative for Muslims because it illustrates the Holy Qur'an in a detailed and practical way. *Sunnah* implements the Qur'anic commands through action and behavior. For this reason, Aisha, may Allah be pleased with her, was reported to have said, "The noble Messenger was the living Qur'an". Therefore, following the *Sunnah* of

the Prophet would also mean following the Qur'an. The
Holy Qur'an clearly instructs believers to follow the path of
Prophet Muhammad:

لَقَدْ كَانَ لَكُمْ فِى رَسُولِ اللهِ اُسْوَةٌ حَسَنَةٌ لِمَنْ كَانَ يَرْجُوا اللهَ وَالْيَوْمَ الْأخِرَ
وَذَكَرَ اللهَ كَثِيراً

*You have indeed in the Messenger of Allah a beautiful
pattern (of conduct) for any one whose hope is in Allah
and the Final Day, and who engages much in the Praise
of Allah.*[39]

It was the noble Messenger of Allah who proclaimed
the truth in all of its purity. Moreover, with a smooth and
clear message, he showed humanity the purpose of existence. In a practical sense, he showed his followers how a
believer should live, encompassing all aspects of life. As
mentioned earlier, the life of no other man in history has
been studied in such fine detail. Although, the noble Messenger lived over fourteen hundred years ago, thanks to
the recordings of thousands of *hadiths*, we have information about the smallest details of his wonderful life. Even
the way he ate, spoke, walked, smiled, wept, sat and stood
up is known to us through hundreds of pages of literature.
After the Holy Qur'an, his life is the greatest evidence to
his Prophethood.

Throughout history, those who have emulated his life
by observing his *Sunnah,* have themselves become luminous illustrations of the Prophet's ever perfect life. Those

---

[39] Qur'an: 33:21.

who have followed the Prophet's footsteps have themselves transformed into guiding stars. The examples of his noble behavior and virtue were reflected primarily by his Companions and those who came after.

Throughout history, those who imitated the noble Prophet's actions have become summits standing taller than Mt Everest. So, *Sunnah* holds the crucial key and strategy of becoming a perfect role model for humanity and an obedient servant of Allah.

Observing the *Sunnah* can also be considered as a demonstration of one's love for the Prophet. Loving the Prophet is an evidence of loving Allah. Evidently, entering this unique triangle of love attracts the compassion and mercy of the Almighty Allah. It is through this love that believers become nominees for an everlasting life in paradise. Therefore, all roads that lead to Allah pass through the noble Prophet. Perhaps, those who disagree with this statement should offer a doctrine better than that of the radiant path shown by the noble Messenger.

History indicates that this would not be possible, because of the simple fact that all man-made ideologies, including doctrines written or proposed by many brilliant minds have failed to bring happiness to humanity. Some of these ideologies did not even accomplish the transition from a theoretical state to a practical one. Carl Marx's socialism is one of the best examples of this. Although, man has the potential to produce doctrines that may help improve the quality of life for human beings, none could excel the teachings of the noble Prophet who drank from the fountain of the Holy Qur'an.

The human soul resembles a seed which has the potential to flourish into a fruitful tree that can yield thousands of fruits and stretch its branches all the way to the eternal paradise. On the other hand, the soul also has the potential to rot away and decompose into the earth. This unique potential cannot be limited or restricted by artificial ideologies.

However, it can be guided towards its true purpose which is to attain the highest level of humanity. The Holy Qur'an and thousands of sanctified scholars clearly indicate that the path of attaining this level of humanity passes through *Sunnah*. After the Holy Qur'an, the *Sunnah* of the noble Messenger is the greatest treasure ever bestowed upon humanity. Only those whose hearts and souls have been blessed with the love of Allah and His beloved Messenger shall benefit from it.

GOOD MANNERS AND
VIRTUOUS BEHAVIOR

GOOD MANNERS AND
VIRTUOUS BEHAVIOR

خِيَارُكُمْ أَحَاسِنُكُمْ أَخْلاَقًا

*The noble Prophet said: "The best among you are the best
in character (having good manners)."*[40]

ood manners are like precious gems. They do not
lose value in any society. Having good manners is
one the most evident qualities of a believer. Allah
loves those who treat their fellow human beings with love
and respect. A true believer loves all creation because of its
creator. It is this love that bestows good manners and well
behavior upon its possessor. Compassion, mercy, kindness,
benevolence, generosity, altruism, philanthropy, chastity,
honesty, trustworthiness and humility are some of the
essential characteristics of a person who has good manners.

When it comes to good manners, no one could surpass
the noble Prophet. Anas ibn Malik, a Companion who
lived with the Prophet when he was a child, describes the
noble Messenger's character in a most unique way:

---

[40] Bukhari: Volume 8, Book 73.

خَدَمْتُ النَّبِيَّ صلى الله عليه وسلم عَشْرَ سِنِينَ، فَمَا قَالَ لِي أُفٍّ. وَلاَ لِمَ
صَنَعْتَ وَلاَ أَلاَ صَنَعْتَ

*I served the Prophet for ten years, and he never said to me,
"uff" and never blamed me by saying, "Why did you do
that or why didn't you do that?*[41]

This is an incredible demonstration of the Prophet's
manners. One can only realize the ascendancy of the
Prophet's manners when one thinks about the number of
times modern parents repeat the words "Did I not tell you
to do this" or "How many times did I tell you not to do
that". Indeed, the noble Prophet was kindest of all human
beings. He would listen and consider the views and opinions of all human beings. On many occasions you would
see the noble Prophet talking to children, listening to their
needs and complaints. He cared for the orphans, widows
and the elderly. When someone called his name out, he
would turn around completely to face the person before
he responded, even if this person was a child. The noble
Prophet was kind and generous to his family, neighbours,
friends and anyone who sought his help.

It is recorded that the Prophet had never said "No" to
anyone who asked something of him. If he had the requested item in his possession, he would give it; if he did not
have it, he would remain silent. The only time that the
noble Messenger of Allah used the word "no" was when he
recited the *Kalimah Tawhid*, "There is no deity but Allah".

---

[41] Bukhari, Volume 8, Book 73.

The noble Messenger always preferred to do his own chores. He would saw his own garments and milk the sheep. The noble Prophet displayed great benevolence towards his household. He would even help his family members with the daily chores. One day, he sat Hasan and Husayn, his two grandsons on his lap and he was kissing them. A Bedouin said, "We do not kiss our children and spoil them like that". The noble Prophet replied, "What can I do, if Allah has removed compassion from your heart?"

The good manners of the noble Prophet were unique because it was Allah Who had bestowed them upon him. Even as a young man, the noble Prophet was given the title of Muhammad al-Amin, Muhammad the Trustworthy.

He was a soft-natured man who treated everyone with utmost gentleness. No one heard a curse word coming out of his noble mouth. He would never tell people's mistakes to their faces. When he saw a wrongdoing, he would speak to the congregation and say, "Some people are acting in such and such way; it is wrong to do this". The noble Prophet was exceptionally forgiving.

During the battle of *Uhud*, a group of archers had left their posts contrary to Prophet's persistent cautions prior to the battle. This in turn had a significant effect on the course of the battle. Believers lost more than seventy soldiers at *Uhud*. After the battle, the noble Prophet did not even say, "Why did you disobey my orders" to any of the archers. He would not admonish or curse anyone. During the same battle, stones and arrows rained upon the noble Prophet. His tooth was broken and he was wounded on the face. He did not even curse the enemy or prayed for their destruction. As he wiped the blood off his face, he said: "O Allah, forgive my people, for they do not know what they do."

It is quite obvious that Allah loves those who possess good manners. Good manners are like a beautiful perfume that attracts the angels and human beings alike. Bad manners are like a dreadful stench that repels angels and human beings. Those who wish to be loved and respected by their fellow human beings should refrain from bad manners. Those who do not possess good manners will never have true friends. Foundations of their friendship will always be based on mutual benefits or interests. Once the benefits vanish, the institute of friendship will collapse.

The friendship of those who possess good manners, on the other hand, is a lasting one. It is not based on material expectations. On the contrary, it is based on sincerity, compassion and love. People who have good manners will make friends at school, at the workplace, in the community and in society at large. They will be respected and revered by everyone. Fethullah Gülen explains this notion as follows:

> Good manners are a virtue and are greatly appreciated in whomever they are found. Those with good manners are liked, even if they are uneducated. Communities devoid of culture and education are like rude individuals, for one cannot find in them any loyalty in friendship or consistency in enmity. Those who trust such people are always disappointed, and

those who depend upon them are left, sooner or later, without support.[42]

One of the most essential qualities of a believer is good manners. Good manners are like a magical key that opens all doors. Good manners can also be regarded as a master key that has the potential to open the eight gates of paradise. The noble Messenger of Allah verifies this with the following *hadith*:

They asked the noble Prophet: "Who are the most beloved servants by the side of Allah?" The Messenger of Allah replied: "Those who possess good manners".

In another *hadith* reported by Abu Darda, may Allah be pleased with him, the noble Prophet said: "Nothing weighs heavier on the Scale of Deeds than one's good manners.

---

[42] http://en.fgulen.com/gulens-works/154-pearls-of-wisdom/1096-bringing-up-the-young.html

NOTES